D0892479

Museums of New York City

Westholme Museum Guides

Museums of Atlanta
Museums of Boston
Museums of Chicago
Museums of Los Angeles
Museums of New York City
Museums of Philadelphia
Museums of San Francisco

Visiting museums is one of the best ways to get to know a city. Westholme Museum Guides, designed for both residents and visitors, are the first-ever uniform compilations of permanent collections open to the public in America's major cities. Each city has its own unique group of museums, some famous, others practically unknown, but all of them are important parts of our nation's cultural life.

Museums of New York City

A Guide for Residents and Visitors

Deirdre Cossman

WESTHOLME
Yardley

Acknowledgments
I wish to thank the many curators, directors, and staff members who graciously helped me in the research and preparation of this book. I am grateful to Bruce Franklin for offering me this project at a time when it was needed most. I would also like to thank Christine Liddie for her copyediting, Katherine Hubbard for her cover photo, and those who offered helpful suggestions and encouragement along the way especially my family, Leigh Hampton, Diana Magnan, Victoria Colyer, Kristine Sui, Dan Reehil, Chuck LaBella, Sarah Davis, Lisa Paulo, and Amy Cohen. And to Mark McDevitt, who understands.

Published by Westholme Publishing, LLC, Eight Harvey Avenue, Yardley, Pennsylvania 19067.

Maps by Joseph John Clark

10 9 8 7 6 5 4 3 2
Second Printing

ISBN 10: 1-59416-009-0
ISBN 13: 978-1-159416-009-7

www.westholmepublishing.com

Printed in the United States of America on acid-free paper.

Contents

Introduction

Welcome to New York City. Whether you are a first-time visitor, a return visitor in search of new experiences, or a longtime resident wishing to know more about the city and what it has to offer, there is much to see and do here, which this small volume aims to highlight.

Museum visits can be extremely personal, so I have tried, where possible, not to interject my personal opinions into the descriptions. I have found that museums are like mothers — protective of their children but eager to show how proud they are of them. While some present their treasures in grand style with lots of fanfare, others are humble and reserved, offering their treasures with quiet deference to those who would take the time to discover them. Large or small, well-appointed or in need of attention, all the museums listed in this guide are worthy of investigation — each has something unique to offer. While New York has many famous museums containing numerous galleries in which to exhibit their vast holdings, you just might find some of the greatest surprises in those quiet little places that often elude attention.

Before it served as a financial center or gateway to the new world for millions of immigrants, New York was our nation's first capital and a city of major historical significance. From the Italian navigator Giovanni da Verrazano, who sailed into New York Harbor almost 500 years ago, to the Native Americans who were the city's first inhabitants; from the Dutch who arrived in 1624 to the English who seized "New Amsterdam" 40 years later: all have left their indelible mark on this great city.

While New York was concentrated in a small area of Lower Manhattan for the better part of 200 years, Greater New York was created in 1898 and is made up of the five distinct boroughs that make up New York City: Manhattan, the Bronx, Brooklyn, Queens, and Staten Island. Manhattan is the oldest, densest and most built-up part of New York City and despite its small size, it is home to most of the buildings, institutions, and neighborhoods that make New York famous. Many of the historic house museums, spread throughout the five boroughs, give visitors an insight into life in colonial New York and remain as proud reminders of the tenacious New York spirit, having served in some capacity during the American Revolution.

Federal Hall, the site of George Washington's inauguration in 1789, stands in the midst of what was then the heart of the city. Today this area is home to the Financial District and offers the visitor a multitude of things to see. Across from Federal Hall is The New York Stock Exchange, the world's largest exchange, which began in 1792 when 24 brokers met under a buttonwood tree facing 68 Wall Street. Around the corner is the Museum of American Finance, the nation's only independent public museum dedicated to the history of the financial markets, and nearby Fraunces Tavern Museum serves as a repository of the Revolutionary period.

What is most remarkable about New York is the peaceful coexistence of these historic relics alongside shining examples of modern technology. The Skyscraper Museum chronicles the modern skyline, forced to move skyward to accommodate a burgeoning city, and explores the function of the skyscraper as a place where people work and live.

In the nineteenth century, New York was the nation's largest city and a preeminent seaport. As shipping became easier, so did manufacturing. Commerce thrived, and the city continued to prosper. The influence of New York as a major seaport can be seen at the South Street Seaport Museum and The Noble Maritime Collection. For a look at how a wealthy merchant lived, visit Merchant's House Museum, New York City's only family home from the nineteenth century to be preserved intact, inside and out.

During this time, industrialists were made; and with that came grander homes, beautiful architecture, and the beginning of New York as a center for the arts. Museums like the Cooper-Hewitt, The Frick, and The Morgan Library & Museum exhibit the art and architecture made possible by this new prosperity. Money was made, and those who had it moved "uptown" and away from the crowded city center. At the same time, the population explosion of the nineteenth and early twentieth century brought more and more people into the city.

Castle Clinton and Ellis Island welcomed millions of immigrants who arrived from Europe in search of a better life. The Ellis Island Immigration Museum, guarded by Lady Liberty, documents the process of the more than 12 million immigrants that passed through its doors. While the streets were paved with gold for some, many immigrants took up residence in the slums and tenements of the Lower East Side. Visitors can observe what tenement life was like at the Lower East Side Tenement Museum, a preserved tenement building at 97 Orchard Street, which interprets the lives of three families that lived there during that time.

New York is a city of immigrants, and nowhere is this more evident than in the vast number of museums dedicated to the culture, customs, and art of a particular people. New York has an abundance of cultural museums to choose from, including El Museo del Barrio, The Jewish Museum, The Kurdish Library & Museum, the Museum of Chinese in the Americas, and the Ukrainian Museum, to name just a few. Others like The Bronx Museum of the Arts and the Queens Museum of Art were created specifically to serve the diverse ethnic communities that took up residence in their boroughs.

New York City is home to several premiere collections. Some are part of larger museums (like The Cloisters, located in upper Manhattan and part of the Metropolitan Museum of Art). The Cloisters is the only museum in America dedicated exclusively to medieval art. The New York Public Library for the Performing Arts—a world-renowned collection that is one of The New York Public Library's four research libraries—is located at Lincoln Center, America's first performing arts center. Home to MoMA, the world's most renowned collection of modern and contemporary art and the Whitney Museum of American Art, a preeminent collection created in 1930 to showcase works by American artists who were overlooked by other cultural institutions, New York's museums present a wide variety of artistic expression.

I hope this small book will serve as a useful guide in making your New York museum experience more enjoyable and memorable.

Using *Museums of New York City*

For the purposes of this book, a museum is defined as a "permanent collection," open to the public, of predominantly non-reproduction artifacts. Some exceptions have been made to include places of note that are free to the public, great spots for children and families and historic places that are worth including that may not necessarily be included in a guide of this sort.

A number of historic homes have been included, not only because they are noteworthy and worth the trip but because New York is more often known as a modern city of skyscrapers—known for tearing things down and rebuilding—than as a city full of relics from the earliest days of the city and nation. There are many other places to explore that have not been covered in this book such as Central Park, which has a multitude of things to see and do. Also, New York Botanical Gardens in the Bronx, The Brooklyn Botanic Garden, the Bronx Zoo—all are great New York attractions and worthy of your time.

The museums in this guide are listed in alphabetical order by the primary name of the museum or collection. Each entry provides the address, phone number, and Web site for the museum as well as the hours of operation and admission prices and policies. Please note that information can change, so calling ahead or checking the Web site is advised. This will also inform you of temporary exhibitions and special programs and events as well as inform you if there are any additional ticketing costs. Some museums have a "suggested" or "recommended" donation policy, meaning that you are not required to pay the amount suggested but it is recommended that you do so.

Others, such as historic homes, keep admission prices fairly low but are often maintained and run by volunteers, so donations are greatly appreciated. Many others are free—a real treat in this city—so a list of those places are indexed at the back of the book. That list does not include museums that offer free admission or pay what you wish on a particular day. That information is listed in the museum entries. Museum membership also offers free entry and is a good option for those who visit museums more often. It offers many privileges like prenotification of upcoming events and exhibitions and special "members only" activities.

Since New York is a city of pedestrians and straphangers, subway and/or bus information is also provided with each entry. While there are parking facilities all over New York City, it can be expensive, and street parking is often difficult, so public transportation is the fastest and most efficient way to get around. In the case of museums on Staten Island, directions are included from the Staten Island Ferry terminal. Consulting the museum's Web site or calling ahead is also advised. Various transportation options are discussed on most museum Web sites. Additionally, New York City's famous yellow cabs are always available and in abundance. Taking cabs can get expensive, but it is always an option and often well worth it at the end of an exhausting day.

Each entry also offers symbols to provide quick reference, such as whether a museum is suitable for children, if it is architecturally significant, or if there is food served on the premises. A key to these symbols is at the end of this section. Following the museum entries is a section that lists museums by categories such as New York Essentials, Museums for Children, and Historic House Museums. Because New York City is vast, there is also a list that categorizes the museums by borough. This is designed to help in planning your visit and assess what is possible to do in a day.

Visitor Information

New York City's Official Visitor Information Center

810 Seventh Avenue (between 52nd & 53rd Street)

212-484-1222

www.nycvisit.com

Open: M–F, 8:30 AM–6:00 PM; Sa & Su, 8:30 AM–5:00 PM

Holiday Hours–9:00 AM–5:00 PM on New Year's Eve, the day after New Year's, Martin Luther King, Jr., Day, President's Day, Memorial Day, Independence Day, Labor Day, Columbus Day, day after Thanksgiving, Christmas Eve, day after Christmas; 9:00 AM–3:00 PM on New Year's Day, Thanksgiving Day, and Christmas Day

New York City's Official Visitor Information Center, as its name states, is the city's official source for information on everything there is to do and see in New York City, including hotels, culture, dining, shopping, sightseeing, events, attractions, tours, and transportation. The center has multilingual visitor information counselors to assist visitors in planning their trip. The center features free brochures, discount coupons to attractions and theaters, and a MetroCard vending machine. NYC's Official Visitor Information Center also sells tickets to Gray Line New York Sightseeing double-decker tours (a stop for the tours is directly in front of the visitor center) and CityPass tickets (www.citypass.com), which is a visitor-friendly program offering six famous New York City museums and attractions for one low price. The visitor center is also home to CityStore, the official store of the City of New York, where you can find all things New York. CityStore sells everything from children's books to silk scarves, T-shirts to subway memorabilia and authentic taxi medallions. There are three visitor information kiosks located in Chinatown, Downtown, and Harlem. They offer additional visitor information for the areas where they are located.

City Hall Park Visitor Information Kiosk

Located at the southern tip of City Hall Park on the Broadway sidewalk at Park Row

Open: M–F, 9:00 AM–6:00 PM; Sa, Su, and holidays, 10:00 AM–6:00 PM

Subway: 1,2 to Park Place; 4, 5, 6, N, R to Brooklyn Bridge/City Hall; A, C to Broadway/Nassau Street; E to WTC/Chambers; J, M, Z to Fulton Street

Official Visitor Information Kiosk in Chinatown

The kiosk is located at the triangle where Canal, Walker, and Baxter Streets meet. It has a red and gold dragon and neon pagoda roof, and there is an 8-foot translucent map of the area on its western wall.

Open: Su–F, 10:00 AM–6:00 PM; Sa, 10:00 AM–7:00 PM

Subway: 6, N, R, Q, W, J, M, Z to Canal Street

Harlem Visitor Information Kiosk

Adam Clayton Powell State Office Building plaza, 163 West 125th Street, just east of Adam Clayton Powell, Jr. Boulevard (Seventh Avenue)

Open: M–F, 9:00 AM–6:00 PM; Sa & Su, 10:00 AM–6:00 PM

Subway: 2, 3, A, B, C, D to 125th Street

Maps

Each museum in this book is marked on the following maps by its page number. These maps are designed to show the reader the general proximity of the museums to one another.

Museums of New York City

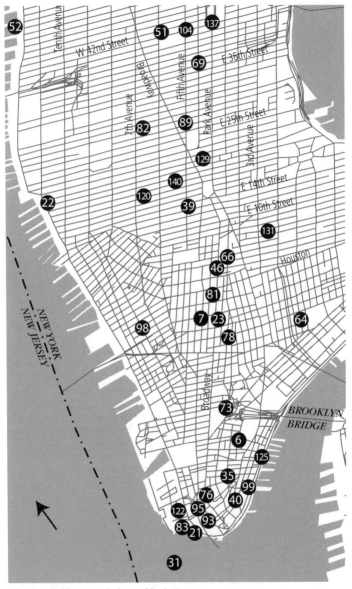

Map No. 1. Museums in lower Manhattan.

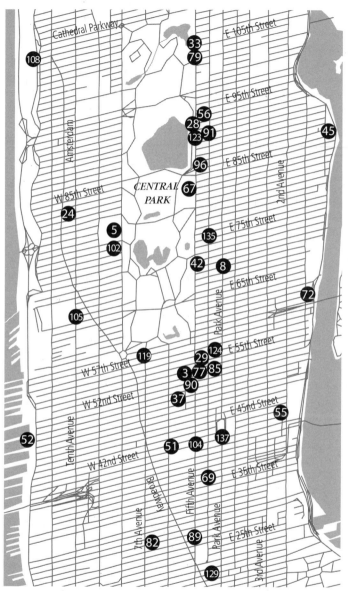

Map No. 2. Museums in midtown Manhattan.

Map No. 3. Museums in upper Manhattan, the Bronx, and Queens.

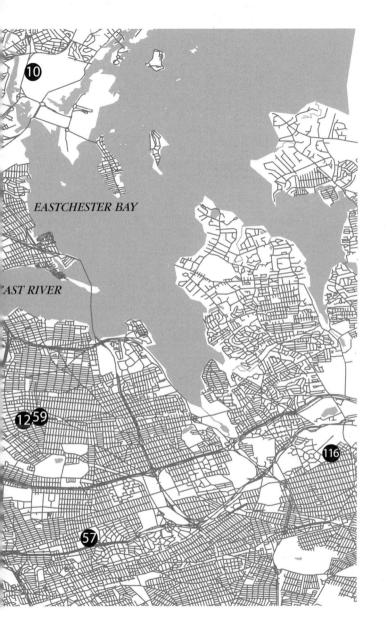

EASTCHESTER BAY

AST RIVER

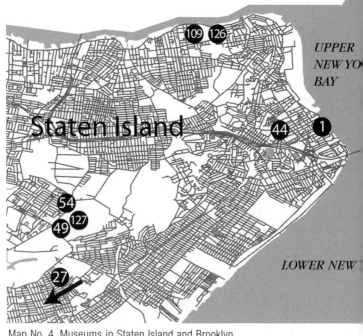

Map No. 4. Museums in Staten Island and Brooklyn.

Brooklyn

BAY

ROC

Visual Codes

Architecturally significant

Exhibits suitable for children

Food available on premises

Must call ahead

Notable art

Notable grounds or garden

Science oriented

Site of historic event

Alice Austen House Museum

2 Hylan Boulevard at Edgewater Street (Map 4)

Staten Island

718-816-4506

www.aliceausten.org

Open: The house is open all year except the months of January and February and major holidays. Th–Su, Noon–5:00 PM. The grounds close at dusk.

Admission: Suggested donation, $2.00 per person; Children 6 and under, free

Directions: From the Staten Island Ferry terminal, take #S51 bus to Hylan Boulevard. Walk one block east to the water.

The Alice Austin House, one of the city's oldest structures, dates back to 1690 and lies on a bluff overlooking New York Harbor and Manhattan on Staten Island. Since purchased in 1844 by Austen's grandfather, it was expanded and named Clear Comfort. For almost 80 years it was home to Alice Austen, one of the first and most prolific female photographers. Best known for her street photography, Austen was also an accomplished artist. Having grown up in a Victorian world, she quickly broke with convention and created her own independent life. Designated a National Historic Landmark in 1993, the house now functions as a museum of Alice Austen's life and the times she lived in and documented through photography. As an accomplished photographer, she started in 1877 and worked steadily taking photographs everyday. There is a new resource room that houses a permanent collection called "Only Austen" that contains 350 of Austen's best photographs. A 25-minute video, "Alice's World," explores her life and photography and is available for viewing at the museum. Additionally, there are rotating exhibits throughout the year showcasing the work of other photographers.

Highlights:

The formal parlor fully furnished in period furniture with some possessions from the Austen family

The panoramic view of New York Harbor covering the Statue of Liberty, Lower Manhattan, Brooklyn, and the Verrazano Bridge

American Folk Art Museum

45 West 53rd Street (Map 2)
212-265-1040
www.folkartmuseum.org

Open: Tu–Su, 10:30 AM–5:30 PM; Friday until 7:30 PM. Closed Monday
Admission: Adults, $10.00; Students and Seniors, $7.00; Children under 12, free
Subway: B, D, F to 47th–50th Streets at Rockefeller Center; E, V to 53rd Street and Fifth Avenue

Founded in 1961, the American Folk Art Museum is a leading cultural institution dedicated to the collection, exhibition, preservation, and study of traditional folk art and the work of contemporary self-taught artists from the United States and abroad. The museum showcases an outstanding collection of 4,000 artworks that span three centuries by giving them a home that embraces the social and historical setting in which they were created. The collection is housed in its first permanent home since 2001. (The magnificent new building, designed by Tod Williams Billie Tsien Architects, is an extraordinary work of modern architecture.) For more than four decades, the museum has been introducing visitors to the story of folk art through its renowned permanent collection that includes furniture, textiles, paintings, sculpture, and pottery and its groundbreaking exhibitions and educational programs. The Contemporary Center, formed in 1997, is dedicated to the preservation and exhibition of works by twentieth- and twenty-first-century self-taught artists. Additionally, the museum is home to the Henry Darger Study Center, the largest public repository of paintings, drawings, books, and archival material by Henry Darger in America.

Highlights:

Girl in Red Dress with Cat and Dog by Ammi Phillips

Nine-foot-high St. Tammany weathervane

Major group of Amish, African American, and New England quilts and other bedcovers and needlework

American Museum of Natural History

Central Park West at 79th Street (Map 2)
212-769-5100
www.amnh.org

Open: Daily, 10:00 AM–5:45 PM; Rose Center remains open until 8:45 PM Friday evenings

Admission: For museum and Rose Center, suggested donation for Adults, $10.00; Students and Seniors, $7.50; Children, $6.00. Admission packages available to include Space Shows and IMAX films

Subway: 1, 9 to 79th Street; B, C to 81st Street

Founded in 1869, the Museum of Natural History explores and interprets human cultures and the natural world through scientific research, education, and exhibitions. The institution houses 45 permanent exhibition halls, state-of-the-art research laboratories, and one of the largest natural-history libraries in the Western Hemisphere. The permanent collection contains more than 30 million specimens and cultural artifacts. The Rose Center for Earth and Space, which opened in February 2000, features the rebuilt and revitalized Hayden Planetarium and outstanding exhibits about our planet and the nature of the universe. The Rose Center structure itself is an architectural marvel that features the largest glass curtain wall in the United States. The Milstein Hall of Ocean Life reopened in May 2003, transformed through current scientific research and cutting-edge technology into a fully immersive marine environment.

Highlights:
The 94-foot-long blue whale model
Fossil Halls featuring two dinosaur halls
The Hall of Biodiversity

American Numismatic Society

96 Fulton Street at William Street (Map 1)

212-571-4470

www.amnumsoc.org

Open: By appointment only; public permanent exhibit at the Federal
Reserve Bank (33 Liberty Street), M–F, 10:00 AM–4:00 PM

Admission: Free

New York is the financial capital of the world, and right in the
heart of the financial district is a former bank building that houses the American Numismatic Society. ANS contains America's
most comprehensive collection of coins, medals and paper cur-
rency from around the world and also encompasses the largest
numismatic library in the world. The collection can be viewed
with a curator by appointment only but nearby, on permanent
view, is an ongoing exhibition called Drachmas, Doubloons and
Dollars: The History of Money. The exhibition, at the Federal
Reserve Bank (at 33 Liberty Street), contains over 800 examples
of the society's most important objects, including the famous
Brasher doubloon. The exhibition explores the different shapes
of money, its function, and the art of money from many cultures
and periods spanning three millennia.

The Anne Frank Center USA

38 Crosby Street, 5th Floor (Map 1)
212-431-7993
www.annefrank.com

Open: M–F, 10:00 AM–4:00 PM
Admission: Free, Donations welcome
Subway: 6 to Spring Street; N, R to Canal Street

The Anne Frank Center USA has the exclusive license in North America to engage in educational and museum activities based on the life and times of Anne Frank and the ideas and ideals found in her diary as well as her other written works. The primary goal of this organization is to motivate young people to embrace moral courage in their thoughts and actions. The center houses a permanent Anne Frank educational exhibit that offers photographs, historical documents, and witness testimonies and includes content at the end of the exhibit relating the lessons of Anne Frank's times to current events. The center also has a reference library of books and videos, a book shop and a virtual tour of the Anne Frank House in Amsterdam. The center has educational and photo exhibitions that have been touring nationwide since 1985 and are available for rental. Additionally, the center offers special events, including workshops, programs, and talks with survivors.

Asia Society

725 Park Avenue at 70th Street (Map 2)
212-288-6400
www.asiasociety.org

Open: Tu–Su, 11:00 AM–6:00 PM; Friday until 9:00 PM; Closed
Mondays and the following holidays: Independence Day, Thanksgiving
Day, Christmas Day, and New Year's Day. Friday evening hours suspend-
ed from July 4 through Labor Day
Admission: Adults, $10.00; Seniors, $7.00; Students, $5.00; Children
under 16 and accompanied by an adult, free.
Subway: 6 to 68th Street and Lexington Avenue
On the weekends, there is a shuttle bus service that goes between the
Asia Society at Park Avenue and 70th Street and the Noguchi Museum.
Buses leave the front of the Asia Society at 12:30, 1:30, 2:30, and 3:30
PM and leave from the front of the Noguchi Museum every hour on the
hour from 1:00 PM until 6:00 PM. The fare is $5.00 one-way and
$10.00 round-trip. Museum admission is not included.

Founded in 1956 by John D. Rockefeller III, the Asia Society is
America's leading institution dedicated to fostering understanding of Asia and communication between Americans and the
peoples of Asia and the Pacific. The Asia Society offers imaginative exhibitions of ancient and contemporary art, often masterpieces from their permanent museum collection. The permanent
collection, donated in 1979 by Mr. and Mrs. John D. Rockefeller
III, contains nearly 300 works that they had acquired over 25
years of exploring Asia and Asian art. This collection of master-
works from South, Southeast Asia, and East Asia dates from
2000 B.C. to the nineteenth century. It encompasses various
media, including bronzes, paintings, and sculpture that reflects

the great achievement and diversity of Asian arts and culture. The society continues to add to the permanent collection by selectively adding pieces of comparable interest and beauty. The Asia Society also offers performances, lectures, films, and seminars to further their mission of presenting the culture of Asia to Americans.

Bartow-Pell Mansion Museum, Carriage House and Gardens

895 Shore Road (Map 3)
Pelham Bay Park, Bronx
718-885-1461
www.bartowpellmansionmuseum.org

Open: W, Sa, Su, Noon–4:00 PM
Admission: Adults, $2.50; Seniors and Students, $1.25; Children, Free.
First Sunday of the month is free to all. Phone ahead for tour schedules.
Carriage house is open April–October. Closed Thanksgiving weekend,
Christmas Day, New Year's Day, and Easter
Subway: 6 train to Pelham Bay

In 1654 Thomas Pell signed a treaty with the Siwanoy Indians for approximately 50,000 acres in what is now the Bronx and Lower Westchester. It is on this land that the Mansion and Carriage House were built in 1842 for Pell descendent Robert Bartow. The architectural scheme of the mansion is original to the house and embodies the Greek Revival style of the period. Most of the furniture and paintings in the mansion are of the period and are meant to recreate an authentic lifestyle but are not original Bartow family possessions. The museum collection includes examples of nineteenth century furniture, especially the popular French and American Empire styles. The property, which is part of Pelham Bay Park, includes nine landmarked acres around the mansion to hike and explore. There are magnificently tended gardens, and the grounds are a great spot for birdwatchers, as they play host to a number of different species of birds, including a rare Barred Owl.

Highlights:

The elliptical spiral staircase in the entrance hall of the mansion

The Lannuier Chamber featuring a bed and crown made by prominent cabinetmaker Charles Lannuier

Authentic Native American wigwam on the grounds

Site of the 1654 "Oak Treaty" between Thomas Pell and the Siwanoy Indians

Bowne House

37-01 Bowne Street (Map 3)
Flushing, Queens
718-359-0528
www.bownehouse.org

Open: While renovations are taking place, the house is available by
appointment only.
Admission: Adults, $5.00; Seniors and Students (high school and older),
$4.00
Subway: 7 train to Main Street (last stop). Walk 2 blocks east on
Roosevelt Avenue, turn left onto Bowne Street and walk 1.5 blocks to
Bowne House, located at the stone wall

Built by John Bowne circa 1661, Bowne House is the oldest
house in Queens and one of the oldest in New York City.
Listed on the National Register of Historic Places and a New
York City landmark, Bowne House is the country's finest example of Anglo-Dutch vernacular architecture, representing a blend
of the two main architectural traditions of colonial New York.
The museum's collections, presently in storage while renovations
are conducted, illustrate the social history of the Bowne family
from the seventeenth through the twentieth centuries. Most of
the approximately 5,000 objects are original to the house and
belonged to the family. Included are examples of English and
American furniture, decorative arts, textiles, costumes, household
artifacts, rare books and manuscripts, paintings, and toys.
Correspondence demonstrates the influence of political, social,
and economic events of the day on the house's residents, including their civic activities. John Bowne is best known for his stand
against Governor Peter Stuyvesant when the practice of religions

other than the Dutch Reformed Church was prohibited. In 1662, Bowne openly defied the ban and allowed Quakers to hold services in his home. He was arrested and imprisoned and then banished to Holland when he would not pay a fine or plead guilty. Bowne successfully argued his case before the Dutch West India Company and Stuyvesant was ordered to permit dissenting faiths to worship freely. Bowne returned to New York in 1664, and the principle of religious freedom was established in the New York Colony. His actions were subsequently codified in various laws that eventually evolved into the Bill of Rights of the United States Constitution.

The Bronx Museum of the Arts

1040 Grand Concourse at 165th Street (Map 3)

Bronx

718-681-6000

www.bronxmuseum.org

Open: W, Noon–9:00 PM; Th–Su, Noon–6:00 PM

Admission: Adults, $5.00; Seniors and Students, $3.00; Children under 12, Free (must be accompanied by an adult)

Subway: B, D to 167th Street/Grand Concourse; 4 to 161st Street/Yankee Stadium

The Bronx Museum of the Arts is a museum of contemporary art that is dedicated to serving its own dynamic neighborhood, the South Bronx, as well as the international art world. Founded by residents in 1971, the museum is located in a renovated former synagogue on the Grand Concourse in the Bronx. The permanent collection focuses on twentieth and twenty-first-century artists of African, Asian, and Latin American descent. Additionally, the museum has a special interest in artists who have lived or worked in the Bronx or whose work addresses concerns specific to the Bronx. Recent critically acclaimed exhibitions include One Planet Under A Groove: Hip Hop and Contemporary Art (2001) and Urban Mythologies: The Bronx Represented Since the 1960s (1999). Throughout its history, the museum has established a local and international reputation as a contemporary art museum that actively engages culturally diverse artists and audiences. As the only art museum in the borough, The Bronx Museum of the Arts is committed to increasing audience participation in the visual arts through its permanent collection, exhibitions, and educational programs.

Brooklyn Children's Museum

145 Brooklyn Avenue at St. Mark's Avenue (Map 4)
Crown Heights
718-735-4400
www.bchildmus.org

Open: W–F, 1:00 PM–6:00 PM; Sa & Su, 11:00 AM–6:00 PM; T, 1:00
PM–6:00 PM during July and August. Totally Tots Gallery (for children
under 5): Wed–Sun, 11:00 AM–6:00 PM as well as Tuesdays in summer.
Closed Mondays
Admission: $4.00 per person; Free for children under 1
Subway: 3 to Kingston; A, C to Nostrand or the C to Kingston-Throop

A trip to the Brooklyn Children's Museum is more like a trip to
the amusement park. The fun starts at the entrance, a bright, old
trolley kiosk in Brower Park from which you descend into this
subterranean museum. Founded in 1899, the Brooklyn Children's
Museum was the first museum created expressly for children.
The Museum offers award-winning exhibits and innovative and
imaginative use of its collection to engage children from preschool to high school. One of the few children's museums in the
world with a permanent collection, it contains 27,000 cultural
objects and natural history specimens. The cultural collection
contains both ancient and present-day objects, including musical
instruments, sculpture, masks, and dolls as well as everyday
household items like baskets and combs. The natural history collection contains rocks, minerals, fossils, mammals, insects, and
skeletons. There is a Children's Resource Center where children
can explore areas of interest in more detail with the assistance of
specimens from the museum's collection. Currently expanding its
facility to nearly twice the size, the museum will incorporate the

latest architectural innovations and is slated to become the first "green" children's museum in the country.

Highlights:

Con Edison Greenhouse and Garden, where children can get their hands dirty with plants, insects and ecosystems

Animal Outpost, where kids can observe live animals eating, sleeping, swimming, and playing

Brooklyn Historical Society

128 Pierrepont Street at Clinton Street (Map 4)
Brooklyn
718-222-4111
www.brooklynhistory.org

Open: W–Sa, 10:00 AM–5:00 PM; Su, Noon–5:00 PM. Please call for library hours
Admission: Adults, $6.00; Seniors and Students, $4.00; Children under 12, Free
Subway: 2, 3, 4, 5 to Borough Hall; A, C, F to Jay Street/Borough Hall; M, R to Court Street

Founded in 1863, the Brooklyn Historical Society is a nationally renowned urban history center dedicated to the exploration and preservation of documents, artwork, and artifacts that represent Brooklyn's diverse cultures past and present. The museum collection contains approximately 9,000 objects dating from Brooklyn's earliest history to the present. Just a few examples are Native American tools, slave deeds, nineteenth-century love letters, a cable-carrier wheel from the Brooklyn Bridge, Dodgers and Coney island memorabilia, and a world-renowned collection of 3,000 Brooklyn-related prints. On display at BHS is Brooklyn Works: 400 Years of Making a Living in Brooklyn, a long-term interactive exhibition about the working people of Brooklyn— their occupations, the challenges they faced, their resilience, and how Brooklyn's workforce contributed to shaping the nation. In addition, BHS launches changing exhibits throughout the year and offers educational programs, neighborhood history guides, community outreach, and its distinctive Brooklyn Walks and Talks series. The Donald F. and Mildred Topp Othmer Library houses a premier collection of research materials on the history of Brooklyn. The collection includes 155,000 bound volumes, 100,000 graphic images, 2,000 linear feet of manuscripts, and over 2,000 maps and atlases. The library also holds genealogies, rare books, newspapers, periodicals, serials, journals, personal papers, institutional records, and oral histories that document Brooklyn's many different ethnic groups and neighborhoods.

Highlights

An original copy of the *Emancipation Proclamation*

The 1955 Brooklyn Dodgers' world championship pennant that flew over Ebbets Field

Brooklyn Museum

200 Eastern Parkway (Map 4)
Brooklyn
718-638-5000
www.brooklynmuseum.org

Open: W–F, 10:00 AM–5:00 PM; Sa & Su, 11:00 AM–6:00 PM; First
Saturday of each month, 11:00 AM–11:00 PM. Check Web site or call
for schedule
Admission: Suggested contribution for Adults, $8.00; Seniors and
Students, $4.00; Children under 12 and accompanied by an adult, Free.
There is an Art & Garden ticket on Saturdays and Sundays for same-day
admission to the Brooklyn Botanic Garden next door
Subway: 2, 3 to Eastern Parkway/Brooklyn Museum; Bus: B71 in front of
the museum, B41and B69 to Grand Army Plaza, B48 to Franklin Avenue
and Eastern Parkway

Housed in a 560,000-square-foot Beaux Arts building designed
by McKim, Mead & White, the Brooklyn Museum is the sec-
ond-largest art museum in New York City and one of the largest
in the country. A big attraction is the new front entrance pavilion and plaza that includes two fountains and was designed by
Polshek Partnership Architects. A must-see for any art lover, the
Brooklyn Museum has an impressive permanent collection that
contains more than one million objects from ancient Egyptian
masterpieces to contemporary art representing a wide range of
cultures. Among the many treasures found at the Brooklyn
Museum is a world-renowned ancient Egyptian art collection (as
well as the equally notable Wilbour Library of Egyptology), an
extraordinary collection of Rodin sculptures, and a major African
art collection. Also notable is the museum's presentation of its

holdings of American paintings and sculptures displayed with related objects from the decorative arts, and Spanish colonial and Native American collections. Highlights of the museum include five paintings by Monet, Albert Bierstadt's *Storm in the Rocky Mountains* and Gilbert Stuart's *Portrait of George Washington*. There is an impressive sculpture garden in the back, and close by are Prospect Park, Brooklyn Botanic Garden, and the Prospect Park Zoo.

Additional Highlights:
Brilliantly painted mummy cartonnage
Asian and Islamic art galleries

Castle Clinton National Monument

Battery Park (Map 1)
212-344-7220
www.npa.gov/cacl

Open: Daily, 8:00 AM–5:00 PM except Christmas
Admission: Free
Subway: 2, 3 to Wall Street; 4, 5 to Bowling Green; N, R to Whitehall
Street. Walk through Battery Park

Castle Clinton was built as a fort shortly before the War of 1812 to defend New York Harbor. Although fully armed and staffed, the fort was never used in battle. In 1817, the fort was renamed Castle Clinton in honor of DeWitt Clinton, Mayor of New York City. The army vacated the fort in 1821, and the structure was deeded to New York City in 1823. From 1824 to 1855, it was known as Castle Garden and served as an opera house and theater until 1854. In 1855, it opened as an immigrant-processing depot, and over the next 34 years, more than eight million people entered the United States through Castle Garden until it was closed in 1890. The building was altered once again and reopened as the New York City Aquarium in 1896 and was one of the city's most popular attractions until it closed in 1941 and moved to Coney Island. Ranger-led tours, lasting from 20-60 minutes (depending on the weather), describe the historic events of the site. Castle Clinton includes museum exhibits depicting Lower Manhattan during the different time periods of Castle Clinton's use and how it affected the development of the harbor and New York City.

Chelsea Art Museum

556 West 22nd Street at 11th Avenue (Map 1)
212-255-0719
www.chelseaartmuseum.org

Open: Tu–Sa, Noon–6:00 PM; Thursdays until 8:00 PM. Closed Sundays
and Mondays
Admission: Adults, $6.00; Seniors and Students, $3.00; Visitors 18 and
under, Free. On Thursdays from 6:00–8:00 PM, admission for all visitors
is $3.00
Subway: 1, 2, 3, 9, C, E, F, V, N, R, W to 23rd Street

The Chelsea Art Museum was created to foster an understanding of postwar originality and to further the language of abstrac-
tion in contemporary culture. The museum provides a venue for
national and international artists who may be less familiar to
New York audiences and offers exhibitions, public forums, and
interactive, multimedia cultural activities to the public. The
Chelsea Art Museum is also the home of the Miotte
Foundation, which is dedicated to archiving and housing the
oeuvre of Jean Miotte and providing scholarship and research on
L'Informel (Informal Art). L'Informel played an important role
in the European and American postwar scene, and Miotte was
an early proponent. Meaning "formless" or "away from form,"
L'Informel is related to Abstract Art. The museum is committed
to scholarship and outreach and important thematic exhibitions
and programs that connect art with crucial issues like the environment and human rights. The museum launches approximately
six rotating exhibitions each year and also has an important selec-
tion of rare books and works on paper.

Children's Museum of the Arts

182 Lafayette Street between Broome and Grand Street (Map 1)
212-941-9198
www.cmany.org

Open: W–Su, Noon–5:00 PM; Th, Noon–6:00 PM
Admission: $5.00 per person; on Wednesdays from 5:00–7:00 PM, pay as you wish.
Subway: 6 to Spring or Canal Street; N, R to Prince or Canal Street

Founded in 1988, Children's Museum of the Arts is New York City's only hands-on art museum for children. The museum was created to give children age 1-12 the opportunity to reach their potential in the visual and performing arts. Children work with paint, glue, paper, and recycled materials to paint, sculpt, build, and imagine. Other attractions include a ball pond to play in and various exhibits to entertain and inspire them. The permanent collection of the Children's Museum of the Arts contains several engaging and interesting collections of art by and for children. Among several collections on display is The Images of Peace Collection, which contains the kites that were made by children in Israel and New York City and flown at a kite festival held in New York in the fall of 2003. The purpose of the project was to encourage a positive, creative vehicle for Israeli and Palestinian children to express themselves and communicate with one another.

Highlights:
Kites from Images of Peace Collection
The International Collection of approximately 2,000 pieces of artwork from children from around the world

Children's Museum of Manhattan

The Tisch Building (Map 2)
212 West 83rd St. (Broadway & Amsterdam)
212-721-1234
www.cmom.org

Open: Summer hours (Jun 21 through Labor Day), Tu–Su, 10:00
AM–5:00 PM; Winter hours, W–Su, 10:00 AM–5:00 PM
Admission: Adults and Children, $8.00; Seniors, $5.00; Children under
1, Free.
Subway: 1, 9 to 79th or 86th Street; B, C to 81st Street

The Children's Museum of Manhattan is home to five floors of
interactive exhibits designed to teach children about art, science,
nature, and the environment by engaging them through active participation. There is a dizzying array of daily activities for children
of all ages, including puppet shows, storytelling, and art workshops.
The Early Childhood Center is an innovative learning space where
young children experience art, music, and storytelling that encourage social skills, self-expression, and language development in a safe,
nurturing environment. The Creativity Lab (for children 4 and
under) provides activities that support early learning in language,
math, and social skills through interactive play and art. For older
children (5 and up), the lab offers hands-on multidisciplinary programs in literacy, science, and the arts. In the computer lab, children 5 and older can use the latest digital imaging technology to
create their own digital designs, while outside, when the weather
permits, children can discover the physical properties of water as
they splash, pour, float, and play at City Splash, CMOM's outside water play area. The museum also offers outstanding performances by musicians and dancers throughout the year.

Children's Museum of the Native American

550 West 155th Street between Broadway and Amsterdam (Map 3)
2nd Floor of the Church of the Intercession
212-283-1122

Open: Oct–May, M–F, 10:00 AM–1:00 PM. Program starts at 10:30 AM sharp
Admission: $5.00 per person. Groups must book in advance.
Subway: 1, 9 to 157th Street

The Children's Museum of the Native American offers a special program that enables children to learn about Native Americans in a creative and interesting way. Each year, starting in October, the Museum focuses on a different geographic area of Native American culture. The program features artifact demonstrations in which children participate in learning how the Indians lived and survived in nature, a puppet show that introduces them to legends, and an Indian workshop where children gather round an Indian dance drum and learn songs and play games. There is also a museum exhibit of photographs capturing the spirit and dignity of the Indian way of life. By presenting the material this way, children participate in learning about the lives and cultures of the American Indians. The museum caters to children from kindergarten to 5th grade, in particular to school groups, and the public is also welcome. It is recommended that you call ahead to ensure that the program is scheduled on the day you are interested in visiting.

The Cloisters

Fort Tryon Park (Map 3)
212-923-3700
www.metmuseum.org

Open: Tu-Th & Su, 9:30 AM-5:30 PM; Fr, Sa, 9:30 AM-9:00 PM.
Closed most Mondays and New Year's Day, Thanksgiving Day and
Christmas Day. Met Holiday Mondays sponsored by Bloomberg are:
Martin Luther King Jr. Day, Presidents' Day, Memorial Day, Independence
Day, Labor Day and Columbus Day.
Admission: Suggested donation for Adults, $20.00; Seniors and
Students, $10.00; Children Age 12 and under are free when accompa-
nied by an adult. Admission includes The Cloisters and Metropolitan
Museum of Art main building when visited on the same day.

Located on four acres overlooking the Hudson River in Fort
Tryon Park in northern Manhattan, The Cloisters is a branch of
the Metropolitan Museum of Art devoted to the art and architecture of medieval Europe. From the moment you enter The
Cloisters, you almost forget that you are in New York City. The
building incorporates elements from five medieval French cloisters—quadrangles enclosed by a roofed or vaulted passageway, or
arcade—and from other monastic sites in southern France. Three
of the reconstructed cloisters feature gardens planted according
to horticultural information found in medieval treatises and poet-
ry, garden documents and herbals, and medieval works of art
such as tapestries and stained-glass windows. Galleries display
approximately 5,000 works of art from medieval Europe, and the
collection is complemented by more than 6,000 objects at the
museum's main building on Fifth Avenue.

The Conference House

7455 Hylan Boulevard (Map 4)
Staten Island
718-984-0415
www.theconferencehouse.org

Open: April–mid-December, F–Su, 1:00 PM–4:00 PM
Admission: Adults, $3.00; Seniors and Children, $2.00

Built in the seventeenth century and located at the southernmost tip of New York State in Staten Island, The Conference House was originally a customs station where British tax collectors could spot incoming ships, appraise cargo, and levy taxes. The building is most noted for the peace conference that was held there on September 11, 1776, and attended by American delegates Benjamin Franklin, John Adams, and Edward Rutledge to negotiate an end to the Revolutionary War. Visitors may roam through the house, maintained in period style, and take in the collection that represents 300 years of American domestic artifacts. The Conference House is the only surviving monument to the manor life of seventeenth-century America.

Cooper-Hewitt, National Design Museum

2 East 91st Street at Fifth Avenue (Map 2)

212-849-8400

www.cooperhewitt.org

Open: Tu–Th, 10:00 AM–5:00 PM; F, 10:00 AM–9:00 PM; Sa, 10:00 AM–6:00 PM; Su, Noon–6:00 PM

Garden entrance on 90th Street open May through September. Closed Mondays, Thanksgiving, Christmas Day, and New Year's Day

Admission: Adults, $10.00; Students and Seniors, $7.00; Children under 12, Free

Subway: 4, 5, 6 to 86th Street

Bus: Fifth Avenue and Madison Avenue buses.

Founded in 1897 by Amy, Eleanor, and Sarah Hewitt (grand-daughters of the industrialist Peter Cooper) as part of The Cooper Union for the Advancement of Art and Science, Cooper-Hewitt, National Design Museum is the only museum in the nation devoted exclusively to historic and contemporary design. With over 250,000 objects, it is one of the largest repositories of design in the world and has been a branch of the Smithsonian since 1967. The building itself, the former home of industrial magnate Andrew Carnegie, is a marvel of design and ingenuity. Completed in 1901, it was the first private residence in the United States to have a structural steel frame and one of the first in New York to have a residential Otis passenger elevator (now in the collection of the Smithsonian's National Museum of American History in Washington, D.C.). Through its collection, exhibits, programs, and publications, the museum explores the vast impact of design on everyday life.

Dahesh Museum of Art

580 Madison Avenue at 55th Street (Map 2)
212-759-0606
www.daheshmuseum.org

Open: Tu–Su, 11:00 AM–6:00 PM. On the first Thursday of the month, the
museum remains open until 9:00 PM. Closed Mondays and federal holidays
Admission: Adults, $9.00; Seniors and Students, $4.00; Children under 12,
Free. On the first Thursday of the month, admission is free after 6:00 PM
Subway: 6 to 51st Street; E, F, V to Fifth Avenue/53rd Street

Opened in 1995, the Dahesh Museum of Art is the only institution in the United States devoted to academic art of the nineteenth and early twentieth centuries. First established in
Renaissance Italy, academic art refers to the tradition of painting
and sculpture taught in the academies, or art schools, of Europe.
This tradition, which involved rigorous training, historical subject
matter, and polished execution, has created centuries of great art.
The museum is built around the collection of Dr. Dahesh, a
writer and philosopher who lived in Beirut, Lebanon. Dahesh
envisioned a museum of European academic art in Beirut, but in
1975 when civil war broke out, friends brought the collection to
the United States. With an emphasis on Orientalism, a favorite
subject of academic artists, the collection of paintings, watercolors, drawings, photographs, and sculptures continues to grow and
enables the museum to explore and define the role academies
played within the larger context of nineteenth-century art.

Highlights:
Adolphe-William Bouguereau's *The Water Girl*
Jean-Léon Gérôme's *Working in Marble* or *The Artist Sculpting*

Dyckman Farmhouse Museum

4881 Broadway at 204th Street (Map 3)
212-304-9422
www.dyckmanfarmhouse.org

Open: Please call or check Web site for current hours
Admission: $1.00 per person and additional fees for special programs
and activities
Subway: 1, 9, A train to 207th Street

Perched high above Broadway at 204th Street, the Dyckman
Farmhouse provides New Yorkers with a remarkable reminder of
early Manhattan. This Dutch Colonial house was built around
1784 and is the last remaining farmhouse in Manhattan. Built by
William Dyckman, it was originally part of several hundred acres
of farmland owned by the family. In 1915, property was purchased by sisters Mary Alice Dyckman Dean and Fannie
Fredericka Dyckman Welch, descendants of the original owners.
They restored the building, one of few early historic restorations
to be undertaken in New York, and they presented it to the City
of New York in 1916. The eighteenth and early nineteenth century furnishings did not belong to the family but are representative of those in the Dyckman family. The landscaping accentu-
ates the beauty of the home and includes an herb garden and a
perennial garden.

Highlights:
Relic Room containing photographs and artifacts
Reconstructed Hessian hut that served as housing for the
Hessian soldiers during the Revolutionary War
Reproduction smokehouse

Ellis Island Immigration Museum and Statue of Liberty

New York Harbor (Map 1)

212-363-3206

www.ellisisland.com

Open: 9:30 AM–5:00 PM (every day except Christmas Day) with extended hours in summer

Ferries run approximately every 40 minutes and operate more frequently during the late spring, summer and early fall. For ferry schedule and group rates, contact Statue of Liberty & Ellis Island Ferry, Inc., at 212-269-5755

Admission: Round-trip ferry, Adults, $11.50; Children 4–12, $4.50; Seniors, $9.50. There is no separate admission fee for Ellis Island and Liberty Island.

Subway: 2, 3 to Wall Street; 4, 5 to Bowling Green; N, R to Whitehall Street. Walk through Battery Park to Castle Clinton, where you purchase tickets. For advance tickets call 866-782-8834 or go to www.statuereservations.com

Ellis Island and the Statue of Liberty are two great symbols of America's immigrant heritage. In proximity to each other, they welcomed the huddled masses from afar and continue to remind us of who we are as a nation. From 1892 to 1954, Ellis Island processed the greatest wave of immigrants in this nation's history. Approximately 12 million people landed here, and their descendants account for almost 40% of the country's population. Fleeing hardships such as poverty, political unrest, and religious persecution, they journeyed to America in search of freedom and opportunity to make a better life. More than 70% landed in New York, the largest port in the country. The government established a special bureau to process the record numbers that were arriving at the end of the nineteenth century. While first- and second-class passengers were processed on board, third and steerage class were ferried to Ellis Island where they underwent medical and legal examinations in the Main Building. In recognition of the significant role that Ellis Island played in American history, the Main Building was refurbished in time for its centennial in 1992. At the center of this restoration project was the construction of the Ellis Island Immigrant Museum, which covers 200,000 square feet and tells the story of the immigrants who entered America through Ellis Island. The museum contains three floors of exhibits and audiovisual displays detailing the history of immigration processing from 1892 to 1954. You can tour the Great Hall, where immigrant legal and medical inspections took place and view artifacts on display such as baggage, clothing, passports, and passenger manifests. There is also an audio tour through the museum that retraces the immigrant's first moments in the New World (available in English, French, German, Italian, Japanese and Spanish. Adults, $6.00; Groups of 25 or more, $4.00 per person). Public tours are periodically conducted by park rangers.

The Statue of Liberty was completed in 1886 and given to the United States as a gift from France. The Statue of Liberty Museum is located in the pedestal of the statue and contains displays and exhibits detailing the design, construction, and restoration of the statue. The statue's pedestal outdoor observation level allows visitors to walk around all four sides of the pedestal offering incredible views of New York Harbor and the Manhattan skyline as well as views of the statue directly above. The exterior grounds offer similarly striking views, and there is a cafeteria with indoor and outdoor seating. The statue's crown is closed at this time. Since it is a popular destination especially in Summer, expect about a two-hour wait for the elevator to the pedestal.

El Museo del Barrio

Heckscher Building (Map 2)
1230 Fifth Avenue at 104th Street
212-831-7272
www.elmuseo.org

Open: W–Su, 11:00 AM–5:00 PM. Extended summer hours: Thursdays,
11:00 AM–8:00 PM. Closed Mondays & Tuesdays and Thanksgiving Day,
Christmas Day, and New Year's Day
Admission: Adults, $6.00; Seniors and Students, $4.00; Children under
12, Free (must be accompanied by an adult). Thursdays, 4:00 PM–8:00
PM are free
Subway: 2, 3 to 110th Street and Lenox Avenue; 6 to 103rd Street. Bus:
M1, M3, M4 to 104th Street (north on Madison Avenue and South on
Fifth Avenue)

The only Latino museum in New York City dedicated to
Caribbean and Latin American art and culture, El Museo del
Barrio presents art exhibitions of contemporary and historical
scope. El Museo was founded in 1969 by Puerto Rican parents,
educators, artists and community activists in East Harlem's
Spanish-speaking el barrio. They envisioned an educational institution that would reflect the richness of their culture. Located
along Fifth Avenue's Museum Mile since 1977, it is well situated
to maintain contact with its core community while reaching out
to a non-Latino audience. The varied permanent collection of
8,000 objects ranges from pre-Columbian domestic and ceremonial objects to a significant collection of works on paper documenting the importance of printmaking in Latin America to
contemporary art installations such as abstract wood sculptures
from the 1970s. El Museo's mission is at the core of the collec-

tions and programs and, while it has expanded, its permanent collection remains a treasured resource for developing a wide variety of exhibitions and education programs. El Museo also offers special events such as film festivals, lectures, symposia, performances, concerts, and festivals that are planned throughout the year.

Highlight:
The Santos de Palo Collection — the second largest in the country

Federal Hall National Monument

26 Wall Street between Nassau and William Street (Map 1)

212-825-6888

www.nps.gov/feha

Open: M–F, 10:00 AM–4:00 PM

Admission: Free. Guided tours offered hourly

Subway: 2, 3, 4, 5 to Wall Street; J, M, Z to Broad Street Monday through Friday

26 Wall Street was the site of New York City's eighteenth-century City Hall. It was on this site that John Peter Zenger was jailed, tried, and acquitted of libel for exposing government corruption in his newspaper, an early victory for freedom of the press. It also hosted the Stamp Act Congress, which assembled in October 1765 to protest "taxation without representation." After the American Revolution, the Continental Congress met at City Hall, and when the Constitution was ratified in 1788, New York remained the national capital. Pierre L'Enfant, best know as the architect of Washington, D.C., was commissioned to remodel City Hall for the new federal government. The First Congress met in the new Federal Hall and wrote the Bill of Rights, and George Washington was inaugurated here as the first president of the United States on April 30, 1789. When the capital moved to Philadelphia in 1790, the building housed city government until 1812, when Federal Hall was demolished. The current structure on the site was built as the Customs House and opened in 1842. In 1862, customs moved to 55 Wall Street, and the building became the U.S. sub-Treasury. Millions of dollars in gold and silver were kept in the basement until the Federal Reserve Bank replaced the sub-Treasury system in 1920.

Highlights:

National Park ranger-led talks describing the history of the site

The Bible that Washington used at his presidential inauguration

FDNY Fire Zone

34 West 51st Street between 5th and 6th Avenues (Map 2)

212-698-4520

www.fdnyfirezone.com

Open: M–Sa, 9:00 AM–7:00 PM; Su, 11:00 AM–5:00 PM (last entrance to the fire safety presentation is one and a half hours before closing time).
Admission: Free for general admission; fire safety presentation admission: Adults and Children, $4.00; Seniors (60 and over), $1.00. Shows are every hour on the half hour. Not recommended for children 4 years old or younger

Subway: B, D, F, V to 47th–50th Streets, Rockefeller Center; 1, 9 to 50th Street/7th Avenue

While not quite a museum, the FDNY Fire Zone is a worthwhile and complementary addition due to its hands-on education and state-of-the-art approach. As part of the New York City Fire Department's Fire Safety Education Fund, FDNY Fire Zone provides a guided, multimedia experience in which to educate the public about fire safety. Visitors can climb on a real fire truck, put on gear, meet a firefighter and learn to identify fire hazards in the home. The Fire Safety Presentation illustrates the power of fire in order to teach prevention and thereby reducing the numbers of fires in the home. Before you head out, hit their retail store that sells the official FDNY merchandise.

Fisher Landau Center for Art

38-27 30th Street (Map 3)
Long Island City
718-937-0727
www.flcart.org

Open: Th–M, Noon–5:00 PM. Closed Tuesdays & Wednesdays
Admission: Free
Subway: N, W to 39th Avenue

Housed in a former parachute harness factory, this 25,000-square-foot museum in Long Island City is devoted to the exhibition and study of the contemporary art collection of philanthropist Emily Fisher Landau. The building was renovated by British architect Max Gordon in association with Bill Katz. It contains an art library, formal meeting rooms, and one of the largest private collections of Modernist furniture by Warren McArthur (1885–1961). Exhibitions feature recent acquisitions and core holdings in photography, painting, and sculpture, including key works by Matthew Barney, Francesco Clemente, Lynn Davis, Barbara Kruger, Agnes Martin, Richard Prince, Kiki Smith, Mark Tansey, Cy Twombly, and Andy Warhol.

The Forbes Galleries

62 Fifth Avenue at 12th Street (Map 1)
212-206-5548
www.forbesgalleries.com

Open: Tu–Sa, 10:00 AM–4:00 PM. Thursdays are reserved for groups,
and advance reservations are required. Closed Sundays & Mondays
Admission: Free. Children under 16 must be accompanied by a parent
Subway: 1, 2, 3, 9 and F train to 14th Street; 4, 5, 6, N, R to 14th
Street/Union Square

Housed in the Lobby of the Forbes Magazine headquarters on
Fifth Avenue, the Forbes Galleries exhibit a broad collection that
showcases the intellectual and playful sides of publisher and collector Malcolm Forbes. Visitors are treated to a wide range of
works in the permanent galleries as well as rotating exhibits that
draw from the permanent collection. Home to the world's largest
collection of toy boats, there are over 500 tin, cast iron, and
paper lithograph toy boats "at sea" and on display. The collection
highlights ships made between the 1870s and the 1950s by noted
toymakers. On display in another gallery are several versions of
the popular board game Monopoly®, including Charles
Darrows' 1933 homemade set, before it was marketed in its familiar form. The gallery of trophies includes more than 175 trophies
for everything from a baby beauty contest to a Tiffany wine bot-
tle holder used to christen a cruise ship. The changing exhibits
draw on the collection as well as borrowed work from other collections and range from presidential papers (a signed copy of the
Emancipation Proclamation in The Forbes Collection) to nineteenth-century French military paintings to decorative arts.

Fraunces Tavern Museum

54 Pearl Street at Broad Street (Map 1)

212-425-1778

www.frauncestavernmuseum.org

Open: Tu–F, Noon–5:00 PM; Sa, 10:00 AM–5:00 PM. Closed Sundays & Mondays

Admission: Adults, $4.00; Seniors and Children age 6-18, $3.00. Please call for guided group tours

Subway: 4, 5 to Bowling Green; 1, 9 to South Ferry; N, R to Whitehall; J, M, Z to Broad Street

Located in the heart of the financial district, Fraunces Tavern offers a rare glimpse of life in New York and America during the eighteenth century. Fraunces Tavern is one of only three buildings still standing in Manhattan that bear witness to the Revolutionary War. From the bombardment of New York City in 1775 when a cannon ball fell through the tavern's roof to Washington's famous farewell eight years later, Fraunces Tavern was right in the middle of the action. Since the local tavern was an important part of daily life in the eighteenth century, these meeting places served both locals and travelers, making them communication hubs and places of business. When the Continental Congress selected New York as its meeting site in 1785, Fraunces Tavern became home to the Department of Foreign Affairs, the Treasury, and the Department of War. With the adoption of the Constitution, New York became the first federal capital in 1789. The Sons of the Revolution in the state of New York purchased and restored Fraunces Tavern in 1904 and opened it as a museum in 1907. Since their founding in 1876, they have been collecting objects relating to the colonial, revolutionary, and early federal periods of American history with a focus on New York. A large part of the collection is dedicated to the Revolutionary period and includes weapons, documents, and historic relics with another portion of the collection made up of art inspired by the events and characters of the Revolution. New York history is illustrated in maps, prints, and newspapers, and daily life in the eighteenth century is exhibited with cooking pots, bottles, and other utilitarian objects.

Highlights:

The Long Room, the site of George Washington's famous Farewell Address to his officers

An eighteenth-century tavern license signed by Mayor Richard Varick

One of Washington's false teeth

The Frick Collection

1 East 70th Street (between Madison & Fifth Avenues; Map 2)
212-288-0700
www.frick.org

Open: Tu–Sa, 10:00 AM–6:00 PM; Su, 1:00 PM–6:00 PM. Closed
Mondays and New Year's Day, Independence Day, Thanksgiving Day and
Christmas Day. Limited hours (1:00 PM–6:00 PM) on Lincoln's Birthday,
Election Day, and Veteran's Day
Admission: (which includes ArtPhone audio guide) Adults, $12.00;
Seniors, $8.00; Students, $5.00. Children under 10 are not permitted,
and those under 16 must be accompanied by an adult
Subway: 6 to 68th Street
Bus: M1, M2, M3, M4

During a stroll through the elegant galleries of The Frick
Collection — a museum housed in the former mansion of indus-
trialist Henry Clay Frick, which was designed by Thomas
Hastings of Carrère and Hastings in 1913 — you will find some of
the most exceptional works of Western art. Ranging from the
Renaissance through the late nineteenth century, the collection
includes works by such celebrated artists as Bellini, Constable,
Corot, Fragonard, Gainsborough, Goya, El Greco, Holbein,
Ingres, Manet, Monet, Rembrandt, Renoir, Titian, Turner,
Velázquez, Vermeer, and Whistler. In addition to major paintings
by these and other masters, the Frick's galleries contain fine
French porcelains, Italian bronzes, sculptures, and period furniture. The Frick also presents special exhibitions that further
enhance the permanent collection. Internationally renowned as
one of New York's leading cultural treasures, the Frick was
established by Henry Clay Frick and opened in 1935. While the

collection has grown over the years, the Frick still maintains the special ambience of an art connoisseur's mansion.

Highlights:

Giovanni Bellini's *St. Francis in the Desert*
Hans Holbein the Younger's *Sir Thomas More*
Renoir's *Mother and Children*
The garden court

Garibaldi-Meucci Museum

420 Tompkins Avenue (Map 4)
Staten Island
718-442-1608
www.garibaldimeuccimuseum.org

Open: T–Su, 1:00 PM–5:00 PM. Closed Mondays
Admission: $3.00 per person
Directions: From the Staten Island Ferry terminal take, the S78 or S52 to corner of Tompkins and Chestnut Avenues

The Garibaldi-Meucci Museum, in the heart of Rosebank, Staten Island, is the historic home of Antonio Meucci, the true inventor of the telephone, and legendary hero Giuseppe Garibaldi. The simple country residence, built circa 1840 in the Gothic-revival style, was moved to its present location where a pantheon was erected over it. Restored and maintained by the Order Sons of Italy, the house contains artifacts collected from around the world. Come and see Garibaldi's famous red shirt — worn when he was wounded in battle — or stop by to see Meucci's telephone models that predate any other patent on the telephone. Also on display are furniture that Meucci made and materials from Meucci's candle factory where both men worked. Dedicated to preserving Italian and Italian-American history, the museum offers lectures, temporary exhibitions, language courses, performances, and annual festivals to entertain and educate the community.

Gracie Mansion

East End Avenue at 88th Street (Map 2)

212-570-4751

www.nyc.gov

Open: W, 45-minute tour starts at 10:00 AM, 11:00 AM, 1:00 PM, and 2:00 PM. Advanced reservations are required for all tours; walk-ins are not permitted

Admission: Adults, $7.00; Seniors and Students, $4.00

Subway: 4, 5, 6 to 86th Street/Lexington Avenue

Gracie Mansion, built as a country house by prosperous New York merchant Archibald Gracie in 1799, has been the official residence of the mayor of the City of New York since 1942. Visitors are given a docent-led tour of Gracie Mansion, transformed into the "People's House" in 2002 with increased accessibility to the public. The Gracie Mansion Conservancy is a private not-for-profit corporation established in 1981 to preserve, maintain, and enhance Gracie Mansion. The conservancy's mission is to raise funds to restore the landmark structure and acquire furnishings that illustrate the rich history of New York, improve the surrounding landscape and gardens, and provide educational services, including publications and tours. Gracie Mansion is a member of The Historic House Trust.

Hebrew Union College–Jewish Institute of Religion Museum in New York

1 West 4th Street (between Broadway and Mercer; Map 1)

212-824-2205

www.huc.edu/museum/ny

Open: M–Th, 9:00 AM–5:00 PM; F and selected Sundays, 9:00 AM–3:00 PM

Admission: Free

Subway: N, R to 8th Street; A, B, C, D to West 4th; B, D, F, V to Broadway/Houston

The museum at Hebrew Union College–Jewish Institute of Religion in New York is a visual extension of the spiritual, cultural and educational life of the college–institute. The museum presents landmark exhibitions, shows for emerging artists, group shows reflecting new interpretations of Biblical texts, cutting-edge exhibitions illuminating the Holocaust and Jewish history, career surveys of celebrated artists, and exhibitions of significant private collections that further define Jewish art in the twenty-first century. The museum's permanent collection, Living in the Moment: Contemporary Artists Celebrate Jewish Time, is an exhibition presenting the renaissance of ritual in our time. It is New York's only permanent exhibition solely devoted to innovative and contemporary Jewish ceremonial art and offers the first significant and comprehensive view in over a generation of the leading artists of all faiths who are creating contemporary works of Jewish ritual art today. This exhibition showcases over 100 objects created within the past decade by close to 100 contemporary artists. The exhibition features select works of ceremonial art that were designed for virtually every key moment in Jewish life such as the life cycle from birth to death, the yearly religious holiday cycle, and the historical, linear progression of Jewish belief. Commissioned especially for this exhibition, these works are available for acquisition.

The Hispanic Society of America

Audubon Terrace (Map 3)

613 West 155th Street at Broadway

212-926-2234

www.hispanicsociety.org

Open: Tu–Sa, 10:00 AM–4:30 PM; Su, 1:00 PM–4:00 PM. Closed
Mondays and major holidays

Admission: Free

Subway: 1 to 157th Street/Broadway

Bus: M4, M5 to Broadway and 155th Street

Housed in a beautiful Beaux-Arts building that was once the
former estate of American artist John James Audubon, The
Hispanic Society of America was founded in 1904 as a free public museum and reference library dedicated to the culture of the
Iberian Peninsula and Latin America. The collection spans the
Bronze Age through the present century and includes paintings
by El Greco, Velázquez, and Goya as well as outstanding examples of sculpture and decorative arts. The library houses thousands of manuscripts and over 250,000 research books. The
Department of Prints and Photographs offers a unique survey of
the graphic arts in Spain from the seventeenth to the early twentieth century. While the collection contains incomparable
engravings and etchings by such seventeenth-century artists as
Ribera, its strength lies in the eighteenth and nineteenth centuries and include almost all of Goya's prints.

Highlights:

The Duchess of Alba by Francisco de Goya
The Little Girl by Diego de Velázquez
The Pieta by El Greco

Historic Richmond Town

441 Clarke Avenue (Map 4)
Staten Island
718-351-1611
www.historicrichmondtown.org

Open: Jan, Sa & Su only from 1:00 PM–5:00 PM; W–F, by appointment
only. Feb–Jun, W–Su, 1:00 PM–5:00 PM; Jul–Aug, W–Sa, 10:00
AM–5:00 PM; Su, 1:00 PM–5:00 PM. Closed Mondays & Tuesdays and
Easter Sunday, Thanksgiving Day, Christmas Day, and New Year's Day.
Interpreter-led tours are conducted daily at 2:30 PM on weekdays and at
2:00 PM and 3:30 PM on weekends
Admission: Adults, $5.00; Seniors, $4.00; Children 5–17, $3.50;
Children under 5, Free.
Groups of 20 or more receive a 10% discount on prepaid admission and
a 10% discount on purchases from the Museum Gift Shoppes
Directions: From the Staten Island Ferry terminal, take the #S74 bus to
Richmond Road and St. Patrick's Place.

Historic Richmond Town is the largest and most complete village in New York City. The 28 historic buildings range in date
from 1695 to 1910, the vast majority of which are landmarked.
Among them is one of the oldest schoolhouses in the country.
The village is made up of residential, civic, and commercial
buildings, including a general store, a mill, a tinsmith, a court-
house, and a museum. The museum has two permanent exhibits:
Made in Staten Island, featuring a variety of objects manufac-
tured on Staten Island (an oyster boat, carriages, and tiles), and
Toys, which covers the art of leisure and all types of toys from
the mid-nineteenth century to the present. The museum also
features one rotating exhibit a year from their 70,000-piece per-

manent collection. Items in the collection include tools, household furniture, clothing, paintings, and sculptures interpreting 300 years of local history. Historic Richmond Town hosts many events throughout the year, including the annual Richmond County Fair, tavern concerts in the winter, and candlelight tours during the holiday season. In the fall they feature Old Home Day in which they interpret the homes and how they were preserved, furnished, and lived in as well as a pumpkin-picking program every weekend during the month of October. In summer they host traditional dinners in which dinner is prepared and served in the traditional nineteenth-century manner. Also offered throughout the year are lectures and seminars on various topics.

International Center of Photography

1133 Avenue of the Americas at 43rd Street (Map 2)

212-857-0000

www.icp.org

Open: Tu, W, Th, Sa, Su, 10:00 AM–6:00 PM; F, 10:00 AM–8:00 PM.
Closed Mondays and New Year's Day, Independence Day, Thanksgiving,
and Christmas

Admission: Adults, $10.00; Seniors and Students, $7.00; children under
12 and members, free

Subway: 1, 2, 3, 7, 9, N, Q, R, S, or W to 42nd Street/Times Square; B,
D, F, or V to 6th Avenue/42nd Street

The International Center of Photography (ICP) was founded in
1974 and is located on a dynamic two-part campus in midtown
Manhattan. It stands among the nation's foremost museums dedicated to preserving the past and ensuring the future of the art of
photography. One of the largest facilities of its kind, ICP presents changing exhibitions of the finest works of some of the most
talented photographers in the world. With over 20 exhibitions
each year, the center presents an extensive array of historical and
contemporary photographs, revealing the power and diversity of
the medium from documentary photography to digital imaging.
The ICP collection includes comprehensive archives of prints and
negatives by Robert Capa, Roman Vishniac, and Weegee, among
others; photographs from the Collection are shown on a rotating
basis in the permanent collection gallery. The School of the
International Center of Photography fosters study of the history,
techniques, aesthetics, and practices of photography in a wide
range of programs: continuing-education classes, two full-time
certificate programs, Master of Arts and Master of Fine Arts
programs in conjunction with NYU, a digital media program,
and lectures and symposia.

Intrepid Sea-Air-Space Museum

Pier 86, West 46th Street and 12th Avenue (on the Hudson; Map 2)

212-245-0072

www.intrepidmuseum.org

Open: Spring/summer (Apr 1–Sep 28); weekdays, 10:00 AM–5:00 PM; weekends and holidays, 10:00 AM–6:00 PM; fall/winter (Oct 1–Mar 31); Tu–Su, 10:00 AM–5:00 PM; weekends and holidays, 10:00 AM–5:00 PM. Closed Mondays, Thanksgiving Day, and Christmas Day.

Admission: Adults, $16.00; Children under 2, free; Age 2–5, $4.00; Age 6–17, $11.00; Students and Seniors, $12.00; Veterans or US Reserve, $12.00; Disabled Patrons (wheelchair), half price; Active Duty US Military, Free

Subway: Trains to 42nd Street to the cross-town bus (M42) to Hudson River

Commissioned in 1943, the USS *Intrepid* served our country for more than three decades and now berths in the Hudson River as the largest naval museum in the world. The carrier took part in the largest naval engagement in history, served as a prime recovery vessel for NASA, and completed three tours of duty during the Vietnam Conflict. Together with the submarine USS *Growler*, the destroyer *Edson*, and over 25 aircraft, the *Intrepid* gives visitors an inside look at life at sea through the many featured exhibits. They range from actual artifacts to installations about current events such as Intrepid Remembers 9.11, an exhibit created to honor those who lost their lives, both the victims and the rescuers. Visit the Virtual Flight Zone, ride in the A-6 Cockpit Simulator, learn about underwater exploration, or just stand aboard the 900-foot flight deck and take in the view of the Hudson. One of the newest additions is the Michael Tyler

Fisher Center for Education: a new 180,000-square-foot, state-of-the-art educational facility built to serve students, teachers, and administrators with a variety of programs.

Jacques Marchais Museum of Tibetan Art

338 Lighthouse Avenue (Map 4)
Staten Island
718-987-3500
www.tibetanmuseum.org

Open: W–Su, 1:00 PM–5:00 PM and by appointment
Admission: Adults, $5.00; Seniors and Students, $3.00; Children 12 and under, $2.00
Directions: From the Staten Island Ferry terminal, take the S74 bus to Lighthouse Avenue (approximately 30 minutes) and walk up the hill.

The Jacques Marchais Museum of Tibetan Art was founded in 1945 to encourage interest, study, and research in the art and culture of Tibet and the surrounding regions. Jacques Marchais (1887–1948), the adopted name of Edna Coblentz, had a passionate interest in Tibetan art and culture—unusual for an American woman of her time. After pursuing a career in the theater, she established an Asian art gallery on 51st Street in Manhattan. She formed a substantial personal collection of art primarily from Tibet, Mongolia, and northern China dating from the fifteenth to the early twentieth centuries. The collection is rich in bronze and other metal statues of buddhas, arhats, and protector deities as well as thangka paintings, ornate ritual objects, and musical instruments. Housed in two fieldstone buildings designed by Marchais in the 1940s to resemble a Himalayan mountain temple, complete with terraced meditation gardens and a lotus and fish pond, the collection is displayed in a setting that is conducive to its enjoyment and its understanding. Special exhibitions, events, and programs are also scheduled throughout the year.

Japan Society Gallery

333 East 47th Street (between First & Second Avenues; Map 2)

212-832-1155

www.japansociety.org

Open: Tu–F, 11:00 AM–6:00 PM; Sa & Su, 11:00 AM–5:00 PM.
Admission: Adults, $12.00; Seniors and Students, $10.00; Children
under 16, Free
Subway: 4, 5, 6 to 42nd Street/Grand Central Station; E, V to 53rd
Street/Lexington Avenue

Japan Society Gallery is among the premier institutions in the
United States for the exhibition, research, and publication of
Japanese art. From prehistory to the present, the gallery's exhibitions have covered topics as disparate as classical Buddhist sculpture and contemporary photography. While there is no permanent collection on display, the gallery presents two major exhibitions each year, working with leading museums in Japan, the
U.S., Asia, and Europe to assemble objects of cultural significance, historical importance, and aesthetic value. In conjunction
with the exhibitions, Japan Society Gallery publishes scholarly
catalogues and offers lectures, symposia, and guided tours. It is
recommended that visitors call or check the Web site as the
gallery closes for a short time in between exhibitions.

The Jewish Museum

1109 Fifth Avenue at 92nd Street (Map 2)
212-423-3200
www.thejewishmuseum.org

Open: Su–W, 11:00 AM–5:45 PM; Th, 11:00 AM–8:00 PM; F, 11:00
AM–3:00 PM. Closed Saturdays & major Jewish holidays
Admission: Adults, $10.00; Seniors and Students, $7.50; Children under
12, Free. On Thursdays from 5:00-8:00 PM, pay what you wish
Subway: 4, 5, 6 to 86th Street
Bus: M1, M2, M3, M4 to 92nd Street

The Jewish Museum is the United States preeminent institution
devoted exclusively to exploring the scope and diversity of 4,000
years of Jewish culture and art. The museum's permanent exhibition, Culture and Continuity: The Jewish Journey, examines the
evolution of the Jewish experience from antiquity to the present.
This vibrant two-floor exhibition includes approximately 800
works of art, archaeology, ceremonial objects, photographs,
video, and interactive media from the museum's outstanding collection exploring Jewish history and culture through art. For over
a century, the museum has presented a wide variety of exhibitions of art and artifacts that are relevant to people of all back-
grounds. The museum also offers gallery talks and programs for
school groups, families, and adults throughout the year.

Highlights:
A diverse display of 38 Torah ornaments of different artistic
styles from all over the world
Leonard Baskin's 1977 sculpture *The Altar*

King Manor Museum

King Park (Map 3)
Jamaica Avenue and 150th Street
Jamaica, Queens
718-206-0545
www.kingmanor.org

Open: Guided tours of King Manor Museum are offered Feb–Dec, Th–F,
Noon–2:00 PM, every half hour (last tour at 1:30 PM); Sa & Su, 1:00
PM–5:00 PM, every half hour (last tour at 4:30 PM)
Admission: Suggested for Adults, $5.00; Seniors and Students, $3.00;
Children 4–16, Free. Groups of 10 or more require a reservation and can
be scheduled throughout the week
Subway: E, J, Z to Jamaica Center. Use Archer Avenue/153rd Street exit.
King Manor is one block north. F train to Parsons Boulevard/Hillside
Avenue. Walk south on Parsons to Jamaica Avenue and one block west
to King Park.

King Manor Museum was the home and farm of founding father
Rufus King from 1805 to 1827 and today is the focal point of an
11-acre park in Jamaica, Queens. King is one of the authors of
the U.S. Constitution as well as one of New York's first U.S.
senators, ambassador to Great Britain, and an early and outspo-
ken opponent of slavery. From the floor of the Senate in 1820 he
declared that any laws or compacts upholding slavery were
"absolutely void, because [they are] contrary to the law of nature,
which is the law of God." After Rufus King's death in 1827,
King Manor went to his eldest son, John Alsop King, who continued the struggle that his father was known for. John was elect-
ed to Congress in 1849 and also became well known for his anti-
slavery convictions. He opposed connecting the admission of free

states to the Union with that of slave states, and as governor of New York State from 1857 to 1859, he fought for the arrest of "blackbirders," men who seized free black New Yorkers and sold them into slavery. John was instrumental in the formation of the Republican Party and cast his vote as an elector-at-large for Abraham Lincoln in 1860. King Manor remained in the King family until 1896, when it was purchased by Jamaica and ownership went to New York City in 1898. One of the earliest historic house museums, King Manor Museum illustrates the story of the King family and the Village of Jamaica as it was over 200 years ago through interactive exhibits and historically accurate period rooms.

Highlights

The Longman, Clementi & Co. pianoforte that Rufus King purchased in England while serving as Ambassador to the Court of St. James

The worn stairs of the servant's back staircase

Kingsland Homestead

Weeping Beech Park (Map 3)
143-35 37th Avenue
Flushing, Queens
718-939-0647
www.queenshistoricalsociety.org

Open: Tu, Sa, Su, 2:30 PM–4:30 PM and by appointment. Group tours must make appointment
Admission: Adults, $3.00; Seniors, Students, and Children, $2.00
Subway: #7 to Main Street, Flushing

Kingsland Homestead, a late eighteenth-century house in Flushing, Queens was built circa 1785 by Charles Doughty, son of Benjamin Doughty, a wealthy Quaker who purchased land on the old turnpike in Flushing. It is surrounded by the two-acre Weeping Beech Park and stands under the shade of the 60-foot Weeping Beech tree, a designated landmark planted in 1847. The name Kingsland derives from Doughty's son-in-law, British sea captain Joseph King, who bought the home in 1801. The two-story homestead has a distinctive gambrel roof, a crescent-shaped window in a side gable, and a Dutch-style front door split across the center. The first floor is used for local history exhibitions that draw on the collections of the Queens Historical Society, which owns Kingsland, and of community residents. The second-floor parlor is decorated as if it belonged to a middle-class Victorian family, and in the hallway is a permanent exhibition of personal mementos such as paper dolls, sewing kits, lace work, and school notebooks belonging to the original families. The Queens Historical Society local history library is housed on the second floor in what was once a bedroom.

The Kurdish Library & Museum

144 Underhill Avenue (corner of Park Place; Map 4)
Brooklyn
718-783-7930
www.kurdishlibrarymuseum.com
Open: M–Th, 1:00–5:00 PM; Su, 2:00–5:00 PM and by appointment
Admission: Free
Subway: 2, 3 to Grand Army Plaza

The Kurdish Library and Museum is housed in a historic brownstone near Brooklyn's Grand Army Plaza and serves as America's center for the study and appreciation of Kurdish history, culture, arts, and contemporary affairs. The library was founded in 1986 and serves as a research institution. It houses books in a variety of languages, periodicals, reports, maps, and clip files and publishes *The International Journal of Kurdish Studies*, featuring scholarly articles on Kurdish history and culture, and a quarterly titled *Kurdish Life*, a researched chronicle analyzing contemporary events and issues. The library's special collections include nineteenth-century maps, periodicals from Kurdish organizations abroad, posters, newspapers, and rare documents, including newspapers from the 1948 Kurdish Republic of Mahabad, a gift of the late Archibald Roosevelt, Jr. The museum, founded in 1988 on the library premises, contains costumes, weavings, and crafts as well as an extensive collection of slides, photographs, cassettes, and videos. The museum also mounts two exhibits per year. The library and museum represent North America's first intellectual repository devoted to Kurdish history and culture.

Highlights:
Photographs taken in Iraqi Kurdistan by *New York Times* correspondent Dana Adams Schmidt in 1963

Iraqi Kurdish costumes donated by Hero Talabani
Kurdish crafts donated by anthropologist Ralph Solecki
Kurdish village jewelry

Lefferts Historic House

Prospect Park (Map 4)
Flatbush Avenue at Empire Boulevard
Brooklyn
718-789-2822
www.prospectpark.org

Open: Apr–Nov, Th–Su, Noon–5:00 PM
Admission: Free
Subway: Q, S, B to Prospect Park
Bus: B16, B41, B43, B48

Lefferts Historic House in Prospect Park is one of the few surviving Dutch Colonial farmhouses in New York City. It was built for a prominent eighteenth-century Flatbush landowner and was home to at least four generations of the Lefferts family. Located six blocks north of its original site, the house is a combination of Dutch colonial architecture and Federal details. Today it is operated by the Prospect Park Alliance as a Children's Historic Museum. The museum interprets everyday life as it was in the nineteenth-century farming village of Flatbush, especially as it was experienced by Dutch, African American, and Native American children from the area. Exhibits combine interactive toys and games with period rooms, historic artifacts, and a working garden that enables kids to experience the cycle of production on a farm. Annual events such as the Quilt Exhibit, Harvest Fair, and Flax & Fleece Fest bring the history of Brooklyn to life with hands-on fun for kids of all ages.

Louis Armstrong House

34-56 107th Street (Map 3)

Corona, Queens

House: 718-478-8274

www.louisarmstronghouse.org

Open: Tu–F, 10:00 AM–5:00 PM; Sa & Su, Noon–5:00 PM

Admission: Adults, $8.00; Seniors, Students and Children, $6.00; Group rate, $6.00 per person. Guided 40-minute tours of the house leave every hour, on the hour. The last tour is at 4:00 PM

Subway: 7 train to 103rd Street–Corona Plaza. Walk north on 103rd Street and make a right on 37th Avenue. Walk four short blocks and make a left onto 107th Street. House is half a block up on the left.

The Louis Armstrong House is a modest two-story house in Corona, Queens, that Louis and his wife, Lucille, settled into in 1943. An international icon, Louis loved his home that served as a haven from life on the road. He entertained friends and neighbors and created a remarkable record of his life through his writings, collages, and home recordings. The house and its furnishing remain the same as when Louis and Lucille called it home. The 40-minute guided tour gives you a sense of the man and the importance of his home life. Furnishings and decorations are original, and the tour includes samples of Louis's private home-recorded tapes and an exhibit area displaying, among other things, one of Louis's legendary trumpets. There is also a large Japanese-inspired garden on view to visitors. The Louis Armstrong House functions to preserve and promote the cultural legacy of Louis Armstrong.

Lower East Side Tenement Museum

108 Orchard Street (near Delancey Street; Map 1)

212-431-0233

www.tenement.org

Open: M, 11:00 AM–5:30 PM; Tu-Fr, 11:00 AM–6:00 PM; Sa & Su, 10:45 AM–6:00 PM

Admission: The Tenement Museum's historic tenement building can only be seen by guided tour. There are public tours (limited to 15 people) and group tours (reservations for 10 or more people that must be made in advance). Tickets can be purchased online through www.tenement.org or by calling 966-811-4111 up until midnight the day before the tour. Tickets may be purchased the same day for public tours at the Visitor Center, subject to availability, but purchasing advance tickets is strongly recommended as the tours sell out quickly. American Sign Language tours are also available on the first Sunday of each month.

Adults, $14.00/$15.00; Students and Seniors, $10.00/$11.00 - price depending on tour; Same day tickets for a combination of tours are available at the Visitor Center.

Subway: B, D to Grand Street. Exit at Grand and Christie and walk east (away from Bowery) for four blocks. Make a left on Orchard and walk north toward Delancey. F train to Delancey Street or the J, M, Z to Essex Street. Once you get off any of these subways walk west two blocks (away from the Williamsburg Bridge) to Orchard Street.

Bus: M15 stops at Grand and Allen Streets. Walk one block east to Orchard and north toward Delancey.

Located in one of the country's most renowned immigrant neighborhoods, the Lower East Side Tenement Museum offers its visitors a look at the immigrant experience through the preservation of an original tenement at 97 Orchard Street. This tenement building, built in 1863, is the first homestead of urban, working class, poor and immigrant people preserved in the country. Between 1863 and 1935, approximately 7,000 tenants called this building home. The Tenement has carefully restored the apartments to interpret the lives of some of these residents to give us a historical look at the life of immigrant families. Other attractions are Windows of 97 Orchard Street, an exhibit that displays artwork in the windows of the tenement, featuring a different artist every six months, the Visitors Center and Museum Shop, filled with gifts and books about the Lower East Side, New York and the immigrant experience, as well as Home Economics: a tenement store, an antiques shop located at 90 Orchard Street.

Merchant's House Museum

29 East 4th Street at Lafayette Street (Map 1)
212-777-1089
www.merchantshouse.com

Open: Th–M, Noon–5:00 PM. Closed Tuesdays and Wednesdays
Admission: Adults, $8.00; Seniors and Students, $5.00. Children under
12, Free. Guided tours on weekends only
Subway: 6 to Astor Place or Bleeker Streets; N, R to Broadway/8th
Street; B, F Broadway/Lafayette

A National Historic Landmark and home to one family for
almost 100 years, the Merchant's House is New York City's only
family home from the nineteenth century to be preserved intact,
inside and out. Built in 1832 and occupied three years later by
Seabury Tredwell, his wife, and seven children, the Merchant's
House gives us a look at what life was like for the family of a
wealthy merchant living in an exclusive residential suburb just
north of lower Manhattan. Gertrude, the Tredwell's eighth
child, was born in 1840 and lived in the house until her death in
1933. Ghosts are rumored to haunt the house. Some say
Gertrude, who never married and died in an upstairs bedroom,
continues to occupy the house. Considered one of the finest surviving architectural examples of the period, the exterior façade of
the house is late Federal, while beautiful Greek Revival interiors
can be found inside. The three floors and eight period rooms
contain the family's furnishings and belongings such as works by
cabinetmaker Duncan Phyfe and possessions like family photographs and articles of clothing, including gloves, hats, and shoes.
The nineteenth-century garden is also open for public viewing.

Metropolitan Museum of Art

1000 Fifth Avenue (at 82nd Street; Map 2)
212-535-7710
www.metmuseum.org

Open: Tu–Th, 9:30 AM–5:30 PM; F–Sa, 9:30 AM–9:00 PM; Su, 9:30
AM–5:30 PM.

Closed most Mondays, Thanksgiving Day, Christmas Day, and New Year's
Day. Met Holiday Mondays sponsored by Bloomberg are: Martin Luther
King Jr. Day, Presidents' Day, Memorial Day, Independence Day, Labor
Day and Columbus Day. The main building including it's galleries, public
restaurants and shops are open from 9:30 AM–5:30 PM.

Admission: Suggested donation for Adults, $20.00; Seniors and
Students, $10.00; Children Age 12 and under are free when accompa-
nied by an adult. Admission includes main building and The Cloisters
(see separate entry) if visited on the same day.

Subway: 4, 5, 6 to 86th Street. Bus: M1, M2, M3, M4 along Fifth Avenue
(from uptown locations) and along Madison Avenue (from downtown
locations)

One of the largest and finest art museums in the world, the
Metropolitan of Art has over two million objects in its collection that spans 5,000 years of world culture, from pre-history to
the present. The two-million-square-foot building is home to a
series of collections, each of which ranks in its category among
the finest in the world. Among them are the Museum's approximately 2,500 European paintings that form one of the greatest
collections of its kind in the world including 5 of the less than 40
Vermeers. The Egyptian art collection's 36,000 objects, most of
which are on display, constitute the greatest collection of
Egyptian art outside of Cairo. The American Wing includes 24

period rooms that display the world's most comprehensive collection of American paintings, sculpture and decorative arts offering visitors an unparalleled view of American history and domestic life. In addition to its vast holdings, the Museum presents more than 30 exhibitions each year, representing a wide range of artists, periods and cultures. Public programs include tours, lectures, concerts, symposia, films and workshops.

Additional Highlights:
Arms and armor
The Costume Institute
Impressionist and post-Impressionist collection

The Morgan Library & Museum

29 East 36th Street at Madison Avenue (Map 2)

212-685-0008

www.morganlibrary.org

Open: Tu–Th, 10:30 AM–5:00 PM; Fr, 10:30 AM–9:00 PM; Sa, 10:00 AM–6:00 PM; Su, 11:00 AM–6:00 PM. Closed Mondays, Thanksgiving Day, Christmas Day, New Year's Day.

Admission: Adults, $12.00; Children (under 16), Seniors and Students, $8.00; Children 12 and under are free when accompanied by an adult. Admission is free Fridays from 7:00-9:00 PM. Admission to the McKim Room is free on Tu, 3:00 PM-5:00 PM; Fr, 7:00 PM-9:00 PM; Su, 4:00 PM-6:00 PM

Subway: 6 to 33rd Street (at Park Avenue)

Originally formed by John Pierpont Morgan in 1924 as an educational institution dedicated to fostering a greater understanding and appreciation of Western history and culture, the recently renovated Morgan Library is one of the few institutions in the United States that collects, exhibits and sponsors research in the areas of illuminated manuscripts, master drawings, rare books, fine bindings, and literary, historical and music manuscripts. Among the many highlights of the collection are the 9th-century Lindau Gospels, three copies of the Gutenberg Bible, Dürer's *Adam and Eve* and drawings by Rubens, da Vinci and Degas. The Library has an impressive collection of original manuscripts by notable authors such as Charlotte Brontë and John Steinbeck and several hundred letters from George Washington and Thomas Jefferson. The Morgan offers lecture series, concerts and special events throughout the year, and mounts temporary exhibitions drawn from the collection to include items not often on display.

Morris-Jumel Mansion

65 Jumel Terrace (Intersection of Sylvan and Jumel; Map 3)
Harlem Heights
www.morrisjumel.org
212-923-8008

Open: W–Su, 10:00 AM–4:00 PM; M–Tu, by appointment only. Closed
New Year's Day, Memorial Day, Independence Day, Labor Day,
Thanksgiving Day, and Christmas Day
Admission: Self-guided visits, Adults, $3.00; Seniors and Students,
$2.00; Children 12 and under when accompanied by an adult, Free
Children from the community may visit the museum free of charge after
school hours on Fridays. Unreserved guided tours for walk-in visitors are
available only on Saturdays at 11:00 AM. These tours cost $5.00 for
adults and $3.00 for seniors and students. Group tours must be sched-
uled in advance due to the limited capacity of the mansion.
Subway: C train to 163rd Street. Exit the stairs at the south-east end of
the station. Walk past the C-Town grocery store and proceed up the
stone stairwell on the left side of St. Nicholas Avenue. The cul-de-sac at
the top is Sylvan Terrace. The museum is at the end of Sylvan Terrace.

George Washington made his headquarters here during the fall
of 1776. It was during this period that the general's troops forced
a British retreat at the Battle of Harlem Heights. The mansion
was built shortly before the Revolution in 1765 by British
Colonel Roger Morris and his American wife, Mary Philipse.
Known as Mount Morris, this northern Manhattan estate covered more than 130 acres and stretched from the Hudson River
to the Harlem River. During the war, the mansion proved to be
a strategic military headquarters and subsequently changed hands
several times before being returned, in 1810, to its original pur-

pose as a country house by Stephen Jumel, a French immigrant, and his wife Eliza. Considered to be the oldest house in Manhattan, the mansion is built in the Palladian style with a second-story balcony and a two-story front portico supported by classical columns. The two-story octagon at the rear of the house is believed to be the first of its kind anywhere in the colonies. The furnishings in the parlor and those in Eliza Jumel's bedroom belonged to the Jumel family, and several pieces are rumored to have belonged to Emperor Napoleon. Through architecture and a diverse collection of decorative arts objects, each room of the mansion reveals some aspect of its vibrant history from the eighteenth through the nineteenth centuries.

Highlights
Stained-glass windows surrounding the doorways of the main entrance and second-floor balcony

Mount Vernon Hotel Museum & Garden

421 East 61st Street between First and York Avenues (Map 2)

212-838-6878

www.mvmh.org

Open: Tu–Su, 11:00 AM–4:00 PM; Tuesday evening from 6:00 PM to 9:00 PM in June and July for Summer Garden Evening Concert Series. Closed Mondays and New Year's Day, Independence Day, Thanksgiving Day, and Christmas Day. It is also closed for the month of August.

Admission: Adults, $5.00; Seniors and Students, $4.00; Children under 12, Free

Subway: 4, 5, 6, N, R, W to 59th Street/Lexington Avenue

Bus: M15, M31, M57

Originally constructed in 1799 as a stone carriage house for Mount Vernon, a 23-acre estate named after George Washington's home, the carriage house was purchased by Joseph Hart after the main house was destroyed by fire in 1826. Hart converted it into the Federal-style Mount Vernon Hotel as a popular country day resort for New Yorkers living in the crowded city at the southern tip of Manhattan. The museum presents the building as a historical interpretation of the Mount Vernon Hotel, which was operated there from 1826 until 1833. The museum is owned and operated by the Colonial Dames of America and is dedicated to the collection, preservation, and exhibition of art, historical objects, and subjects pertaining to the hotel. A particular focus is America in the first half of the nineteenth century, particularly the hotel industry, the pursuit of leisure and travel and customs of Americans within the context of New York history.

Municipal Archives of the City of New York

31 Chambers Street, Room 103 (Map 1)

212-NEW-YORK or 311

www.nyc.gov/records

Open: M–Th, 9:00 AM–4:30 PM; F, 9:00 AM–1:00 PM. Closed on public holidays

Admission: Free

Subway: 4, 5, 6 to Brooklyn Bridge; N, R to City Hall; 1, 2, 3, 9 to Chambers Street

Founded in 1950, the Municipal Archives preserves and makes available the historical records created by the government of the City of New York. With materials dating from 1647 to the present, the Municipal Archives has approximately 160,000 cubic feet of manuscript materials, photographs, moving images, sound recordings, architectural records, maps, and office records. The archives has significant records relevant to the city's infrastructure, including parks, bridges, buildings, and streets such as John Roebling's original plans for the construction of the Brooklyn Bridge and Frederick Law Olmsted's plans for Central Park. The archives holds records of the mayors' office dating from 1849 to the present and a collection of records pertaining to the administration of criminal justice dating from 1684 to 1966, which constitutes the largest and most comprehensive collection of such material in the English-speaking world. Also of interest are vital records, census, and city directories—essential for conducting family history research. There are more than one million photographic images in 50 collections offering visitors a rare pictorial history of the city. Some of the most recognizable New York photographs are housed here, and copies are available for purchase.

Museum for African Art

36-01 43rd Avenue (Map 3)
Long Island City
718-784-7700
www.africanart.org

Open: M, Th, F, 10:00 AM–5:00 PM; Sa & Su, 11:00 AM–5:00 PM.
Closed Tuesdays and Wednesdays
Admission: Adults, $6.00; Seniors, Students and Children, $3.00;
Children under 6, Free. Mondays, Thursdays, and Fridays from 10:00
AM–11:00 AM are free for all
Subway: 7 to 33rd Street
Bus: Q32 to 35th Street and Queens Boulevard; Q60 to 33rd Street and
Queens Boulevard

Founded in 1984, the Museum for African Art was created to
increase understanding and appreciation of Africa's ancient and
modern cultures. It is the only independent institution in the
United States devoted to organizing and circulating exhibitions
of traditional and contemporary African art of the highest aesthetic and scholarly quality. For 20 years, the museum's exhibitions have profoundly changed and deepened people's understanding of Africa and African art. Founded in the belief that
traditional African art is among mankind's highest achievements,
the museum continues to develop original and innovative
approaches to the arts of the African continent. Currently located in an interim space in Long Island City, the Museum for
African Art is building a new permanent home on Manhattan's
Museum Mile at 110th Street and Fifth Avenue. While there is
no permanent collection on display at this site, the temporary
exhibitions cover a wide variety of topics in which to explore the

art of the African culture. Past exhibitions have included Face of the Gods: Art and Altars of Africa and the African Americans; Art that Heals: The Image as Medicine in Ethiopia; and Looking Both Ways: Art of the Contemporary African Diaspora. Additionally, the museum is a major publisher of books on African art and presents educational programs, lectures, workshops, and performances for children, students, and adults.

Museum of American Finance

28 Broadway at Bowling Green Park (Map 1)
212-908-4110
www.financialhistory.org
Open: Tu–Sa, 10:00 AM–4:00 PM. Closed Sundays and Mondays and
federal and stock market holidays
Admission: $2.00 per person
Subway: 1, 9 to Rector Street; 2, 3 to Wall Street; 4, 5 to Bowling Green;
N, R to Whitehall Street; J, M to Broad Street

The Museum of American Finance is the nation's only independent public museum dedicated to the history of the financial
markets. Its permanent collection includes 10,000 financial documents and artifacts such as stocks, bonds, photographs, and other
finance-related pieces. Permanent collection exhibitions are often
organized and displayed to commemorate significant historical
anniversaries and events. Recent examples have included the centennial anniversary of aviation and the 50th anniversary of the
Small Business Administration. Among the objects on display is
the first dollar sign used on a federal document, a bond issued to
and signed by George Washington, the earliest photograph of
Wall Street from the 1860s, and numerous artifacts from the
crash of 1929. There is a working stock ticker—a replica of what
was used in late 1800s through the crash of 1929—where visitors
can make a souvenir of their visit. Financial education is the
focus of the museum, and it is an affiliate of the Smithsonian
Institution. The museum also organizes business and finance
exhibits that change every six months and cover everything from
counterfeiting to piggybanks to the history of the Dow.

Museum of Arts & Design

40 West 53rd Street (between Fifth and Avenue of the Americas; Map 2)
212-956-3535
www.madmuseum.org

Open: Daily, 10:00 AM–6:00 PM; Thursdays, 10:00 AM–8:00 PM
Admission: Adults, $9.00; Seniors and Students, $6.00; Children under
12, Free; on Thursdays from 6:00 PM to 8:00 PM, pay what you wish
Subway: E, V to Fifth Avenue; B, D to 7th Avenue; N, R to 49th Street; Q
to Rockefeller Center

The Museum of Arts & Design is the country's leading cultural
institution dedicated to the collection and exhibition of contemporary objects created in a wide range of mediums, including
clay, glass, wood, metal, and fiber. The museum celebrates materials and processes that today are embraced by practitioners in the
fields of craft, decorative arts, and design. MAD's distinguished
permanent collection includes more than 2,000 objects by
renowned and emerging artists and designers from around the
world. Representing many forms of creativity and craftsmanship,
the collection focuses on contemporary sculptural or functional
objects. The museum offers Thursday-evening adult lectures and
panel discussions, Saturday studio demonstrations, Sunday after-
noon family workshops, gallery tours with curators, meet-the-
artists evenings, and special programs for schools and educators.
The store at the museum offers unusual, well-designed objects
made by hand, including jewelry, glass, wearables, home accessories, and many intriguing gift items. The museum will move to
a new 54,000-square-foot building at Two Columbus Circle in
Manhattan in 2007. There the museum will be able to display
works from its permanent collection in dedicated galleries.

Museum of Chinese in the Americas

70 Mulberry Street at the corner of Bayard Street, 2nd Floor (Map 1)
212-619-4785
www.moca-nyc.org

Open: Tu–Su, Noon–6:00 PM; Fridays until 7:00 PM. Closed Mondays
Call for holiday schedules.
Admission: Suggested donation for Adults, $3.00; Seniors and Students,
$1.00; Children under 12, Free. Fridays are free all day. Fees vary for
groups, please call.
Subway: 6, N, R, Q, W, J, M, Z to Canal Street
Bus: M15 and M104 to Chinatown

Located downtown on the second floor of the historic building
that once housed P.S. 23 in the heart of Chinatown, the
Museum of Chinese in the Americas is the first full-time, pro-
fessionally staffed museum dedicating to preserving and interpreting the history and culture of Chinese and their descendants in
the Western Hemisphere. MoCA began as a community-based
organization founded in 1980 by Jack Tchen, Charlie Lai, and
Chinese American artists, historians, and students who felt that
the memories of first-generation "old timers" would be lost
without oral history, photo documentation, research, and collection efforts. After more than 20 years of collecting artifacts and
archival materials, the museum has become the most important
national archives of materials about Chinese life in America.
Exhibits reflect the perspective of the Chinese American experience within the greater context of the history of the Americas,
which makes it interesting and accessible to all visitors. As a
result of this great endeavor, MoCA has become the keeper of
the community's documented history as well its cultural history.

Museum of the City of New York

1220 Fifth Avenue at 103rd Street (Map 2)

212-534-1672

www.mcny.org

Open: Tu–Su, 10:00 AM–5:00 PM. Closed Mondays except holidays that fall on Mondays

Admission: Adults, $7.00; Students, Seniors, and Children, $5.00; Adults with children, $15.00

Subway: 6 to 103rd Street, walk 3 blocks west; 2, 3 to 110th Street and Lenox Avenue, walk one block east to Fifth Avenue and south to 103rd Street.

A treasure trove of New York history can be found at the Museum of the City of New York. The vast collection of more than one and a half million pieces includes paintings, photographs, costumes, toys, rare books, manuscripts, sculptures, decorative arts objects, and other artifacts. The museum has one of the most important photographic collections and the finest and most complete collection of Currier & Ives hand-colored lithographs. One of the strongest historically based collections of clothing in the country, the Costume Collection has over 25,000 garments and accessories worn by New Yorkers from the mid-eighteenth century to the present. Also at home here is a world-renowned collection on American theater, including original set and costume renderings, posters, original play scripts, and more than 5,000 costumes and props. The museum has three long-term exhibitions on view: a history of the ports of New York City, fire prevention and protection, and a history of Broadway. The museum also launches eight special exhibitions per year drawing from their collection and incorporating artifacts on loan to the museum and offers year-round public programs.

Additional Highlights:

The Stettheimer Dollhouse—created in the 1920s, this three-dimensional work of art contains an art gallery with original works of art by twentieth-century modern artists

Museum of Comic and Cartoon Art

594 Broadway (between Houston & Prince Streets; Map 1)
Suite 401
212-254-3511
www.moccany.org

Open: F–M, Noon–5:00 PM; Tu & Th by appointment
Admission: General, $3.00; Children 12 and under, Free
Subway: 6, B, D, F, V to Broadway/Lafayette; N, R, W to Prince Street

The Museum of Comic and Cartoon Art (MoCCA) was created for the collection, preservation, education, study, and display
of comic and cartoon art. Cartoons and comics have been instrumental in documenting and interpreting historic events, and the
museum explores, through its education programs, exhibitions,
and collection, its artistic, historical, and cultural impact. The
museum aims to educate the public about comic and cartoon art,
how it is crafted, and how it reflects history. The museum's permanent collection is continuing to grow from donations of artwork. Pieces range from Academy Award®–nominated animation to historic political cartoons; award-winning comic book art
to Pulitzer Prize newspaper strips. Exhibitions are launched on a
regular basis and usually feature pieces from the permanent collection. The museum hosts MoCCA Mondays, a weekly scheduled event of guests, lectures, and programs related to comic and
cartoon art. For upcoming events, please call or check the
MoCCA Web site.

Museum at FIT–Fashion Institute of Technology

Seventh Avenue at 27th Street, E Building (Map 1)

212-217-5970

www.fitnyc.edu\museum

Open: Tu–F, Noon–8:00 PM; Sa, 10:00 AM–5:00 PM. Closed Sundays

Admission: Free

Subway: 1, 9, C, E, N, R, V to 28th Street

Since New York is one of the fashion capitals of the world, it is fitting that the Fashion Institute of Technology, a premier fashion school, is the repository for one of the world's most important collections of costumes and textiles. The collections are actively used by faculty and students as well as textile, fashion, and accessory designers and other industry professionals. Dedicated to documenting fashion and style, the museum features rotating exhibits covering various themes and showcasing six different exhibits per year. Exhibitions have run the gamut from a retrospective on a fashion photographer to the connection between fragrance and fashion to a celebration of Seventh Avenue and American fashion design. The variety and depth of what is offered lends insight into the significance and influence of fashion and style at every social level.

Museum of Jewish Heritage–A Living Memorial to the Holocaust

36 Battery Place (Map 1)

646-437-4200

www.mjhnyc.org

Open: Su–Tu, Th, 10:00 AM–5:45 PM; W, 10:00 AM–8:00 PM; F, 10:00 AM–5:00 PM (during Daylight Savings Time); Friday and the eve of Jewish holidays, 10:00 AM–3:00 PM. Closed Saturdays, Jewish holidays, and Thanksgiving Day

Admission: Adults, $10.00; Seniors, $7.00; Students, $5.00; Children 12 and under, Free

The Museum of Jewish Heritage–A Living Memorial to the Holocaust honors those who died by celebrating their lives and the legacy that they left behind. The museum's 30,000-square-foot symbolic six-sided shape and tiered roof are a reminder of the six million who perished in the Holocaust as well as a representation of the Star of David. The museum's core exhibition of personal objects, photographs, and original films illustrate the story of the Jewish heritage in the twentieth century. The 2,000 photographs, 800 historical and cultural artifacts, and 24 original documentary films in the museum's core exhibition represent a small portion of the museum's 15,000 objects. The collection is organized around three chronological themes: Jewish Life a Century Ago, The War Against the Jews, and Jewish Renewal, each on a separate floor to best illustrate the Jewish experience from the 1880s to the present. The museum develops special exhibitions and public programs to examine more closely specific areas of Jewish history and heritage. The 82,000-square-foot Robert M. Morgenthau Wing contains the state-of-the-art

Edmond J. Safra Hall, catering hall, classrooms, a resource center, and expanded gallery space for special exhibitions.

Highlights:

Andy Goldsworthy's first permanent commission in New York City, *Garden of Stones*, is a memorial garden of trees growing out of stone

The Museum of Modern Art

11 West 53rd Street (Map 2)
212-708-9400
www.moma.org

Open: W, Th, 10:30 AM–5:30 PM; F, 10:30 AM–8:00 PM; Sa–M, 10:30
AM–5:30 PM. Closed Tuesdays and Thanksgiving Day and Christmas Day
Admission: Adults, $20.00; Seniors, $16.00; Students, $12.00; Children
16 and under and accompanied by an adult, Free. Admission is free for
all visitors during Target Free Friday Nights, every Friday evening from
4:00 PM to 8:00 PM. Tickets for Target Free Friday Nights are not avail-
able in advance. Film tickets for same-day screenings are available at no
charge by presenting your museum admission ticket stub at the Film and
Media Desk.
Subway: E, V to Fifth Avenue/53rd Street; B, D, F to 47/50th
Streets/Rockefeller Center
Bus: M1, M2, M3, M4, M5 to 53rd Street

A recent major transformation of MoMA's renowned midtown
building by Japanese architect Yoshio Taniguchi has expanded
upon and incorporated the original 1939 International Style
building by Goodwin and Stone and Philip Johnson's 1953 addition to create a magnificent 630,000-square-foot museum in
which to experience all that MoMA has to offer. Founded in
1929 with the intention of establishing an institution devoted
exclusively to modern art, the collection of the Museum of
Modern Art constitutes the world's most renowned collection of
modern and contemporary art. From an initial gift of eight prints
and one drawing, the collection has grown to include over
150,000 paintings, sculptures, drawings, prints, photographs,
architectural models and drawings, and design objects.

Enhancements include new galleries for the display of works of contemporary art from the permanent collection and a new gallery for the display of video and new media. The museum offers an active schedule of temporary exhibitions addressing a wide range of subjects, mediums, and time periods, highlighting significant developments in the visual arts and new interpretations of major artists and art historical movements. The museum also presents film programs, gallery talks, lectures, symposia, and special activities for parents, teachers, families, students, preschoolers, bilingual visitors, and visitors with special needs. The new museum provides three retail shops (MoMA Design and Book Store, MoMA Books, and an exhibition shop), a new fine dining restaurant (The Modern), a casual restaurant and bar (The Bar Room), and Café 2 and Terrace 5 (operated by Danny Meyer's Union Square Hospitality Group).

Additional Highlights:
van Gogh's *The Starry Night*
Matisse's *Dance (I)*
Klimt's *Hope, II*
Dali's *The Persistence of Memory*
The Abby Aldrich Rockefeller Sculpture Garden

Museum of the Moving Image

35th Avenue at 36th Street (Map 3)
Astoria, Queens
718-784-0077
www.movingimage.us

Open: W–Th, Noon–5:00 PM; F, Noon–8:00 PM (free after 4:00 PM); Sa
& Su, 11:00 AM–6:30 PM. Call or check Web site for special hours for
holidays and school breaks
Admission: Adults, $10.00; Students and Seniors, $7.50; Children 5–18,
$5.00; Children under 5, free
Subway: Weekdays, R, V to Steinway Street; weekends, R, G to Steinway
Street

The Museum of the Moving Image is dedicated to educating
the public about the art, history, technique, and technology of
film, television and digital media and its impact on culture and
society. Housed in a former movie studio built for Paramount in
1920, the museum has the nation's largest and most comprehensive holdings of moving image artifacts—one of the most important collections of its kind in the world—with more than
100,000 items. The collection includes photographed studies of
locomotion from 1887, an early mechanical television from 1931,
and the chariot driven by Charlton Heston in the 1959 epic film
Ben Hur. The museum owns artifacts from every stage of pro-
ducing, promoting, and exhibiting motion pictures and television
and has exceptional collections of television sets, licensed merchandise, rare photographs, and video and computer games.
Regularly revised and updated, the museum's core exhibition,
Behind the Screen, spans two floors and 14,000 square feet and
uses historical artifacts, commissioned art works, video clips,

interviews, and interactive exhibits to provide a look at how moving images are produced, marketed, and exhibited. Its interactive exhibits invite visitors to make animation, select sound effects, and create flipbooks for themselves, among other activities. In an effort to expand public understanding of and appreciation for film, television, and digital media, the museum offers exhibitions, screenings and seminars and education programs. The museum has also been a pioneer in offering online exhibitions such as The Living Room Candidate, a history of presidential campaign commercials.

The Museum of Sex

233 Fifth Avenue at 27th Street (Map 2)
212-689-6337
www.museumofsex.com
Open: Su–F, 11:00 AM–6:30 PM; Sa, 11:00 AM–8:00 PM. Last ticket sold 45 minutes before closing
Admission: Adults, $14.50 + tax; Seniors and Students, $13.50 + tax; Group visits are also available. Tickets may be purchased in advance online or by calling 866-MOSEXTIX. There is a $1.50 per-ticket service charge for tickets purchased online or by phone.
Subway: 6 to 28th Street; N, R to 28th Street
Bus: M2, M3, M5 (down Fifth Avenue); M6, M7 (down Broadway)

The Museum of Sex has a mission to preserve and present the history, evolution, and cultural significance of human sexuality, and at the heart of the museum is the exhibition Spotlight on the Permanent Collection. The exhibition offers a sampling of American objects and ephemera drawn from over 10,000 items in the museum's permanent collection. Spotlight explores themes such as sex education, sex in art, law and public morality, sex in advertising, sex and entertainment, and the significance of the Museum of Sex in New York City. Highlights of the sex and technology collection include homemade contraptions and commercial devices registered with the U.S. Patent Office that prevent, improve, or enhance sexual function. The exhibition includes erotic works by well-known artists like Randy Wray, Gerald Gooch, and Alex Rockman that were donated to the museum. Other unique items on display include an antique chastity belt, early twentieth-century sex-education pamphlets, and visual erotica, including 3-D Hollywood images. Additionally, the museum offers a rotating exhibition series and public programming.

The Museum of Television & Radio

25 West 52nd Street (Map 2)

212-621-6800

www.mtr.org

Open: Tu–Su, Noon–6:00 PM; Thursday evenings until 8:00 PM. Closed
Mondays and New Year's Day, Independence Day, Thanksgiving Day, and
Christmas Day

Admission: Adults, $10.00; Students and Seniors, $8.00; Children under
14, $5.00

Subway: E, V to Fifth Avenue and 53rd Street; N, R, W to 49th Street and
Seventh Avenue; 1, 9 to 50th Street and Broadway; B, D, F to 47th-50th
Street/Rockefeller Center

The Museum of Television & Radio was founded by William S.
Paley in 1975 to collect, preserve, and interpret television and
radio programming and to make these programs available to the
public. Located in both New York and Los Angeles, its international collection of over 100,000 programs covers more than 80
years of television and radio history. From the lost *Honeymooners*
episode to the first moonwalk to Apple Computer's famed 1984
commercial, there are plenty of interesting options. Both sites
house identical collections that include news, public-affairs programs and documentaries, performing-arts programs, children's
programming, sports, comedy and variety shows, and commercial
advertising. Each year, the museum organizes screenings and lis-
tening series, seminars, and education classes using programs from
the collection. Visitors can view or listen on individual consoles;
attend a screening exhibition in a theater; attend a family workshop or seminar featuring performers, directors, writers, and pro-
ducers; or see a live radio broadcast in the museum's radio studios.

National Academy Museum

1083 Fifth Avenue at 89th Street (Map 2)
212-369-4880
www.nationalacademy.org

Open: W–Th, Noon–5:00 PM; F–Su, 11:00 AM–6:00 PM; Closed
Mondays & Tuesdays and public holidays
Admission: Adults, $10.00; Students, Seniors and Children under 16,
$5.00. Groups of ten or more, $8.00 per person. Guided tours: Docent-
led public tours are offered every Friday at 2:00 PM. Admission: $5.00
per person plus $25.00 tour fee for up to 15 adults; $40.00 tour fee for
up to 50 adults. School group admission: $50.00 tour fee for up to 40
students
Subway: 4, 5, 6 to Lexington and 86th Street

Housed in a beautiful Beaux-Arts townhouse along Fifth
Avenue's Museum Mile, the academy is home to one of the
largest public collections of nineteenth-, twentieth-, and twenty-
first-century American art in the country. The mansion, into
which the academy moved in 1942, was originally the home of
Archer Milton Huntington (1870–1955), heir to the fortune
amassed by his father, railroad magnate Collis Huntington, and
his wife, the sculptor Anna Hyatt Huntington (1876–1973). In
1902, Huntington purchased several properties along Fifth
Avenue between 89th and 90th Streets, including a small house
at 1083. He hired the architect and interior designer Ogden
Codman, Jr. to enlarge the house and turn it into the mansion
that stands today. The Huntingtons lived in the house until 1939
when they gave the building and the surrounding properties to
the National Academy. The academy is an honorary association
of professional artists that maintains a museum and an art school.

A requirement of membership is the contribution of a representative example of each artist's work. Since its founding in 1825, the academy has amassed an impressive collection of American paintings, sculptures, prints, and architectural representations forming a permanent collection of over 8,000 works in almost every artistic style from the nineteenth century on.

Highlights:

Works by artists/members, including William Merritt Chase, Frank Gehry, Jasper Johns, and John Singer Sargent

National Museum of the American Indian

George Gustav Heye Center (Map 1)
One Bowling Green
212-514-3700
www.AmericanIndian.si.edu

Open: Daily, 10:00 AM–5:00 PM; Thursdays until 8:00 PM
Admission: Free
Subway: 1,9 to South Ferry; 2, 3 to Wall Street; 4, 5 to Bowling Green;
R, W to Whitehall Street; J, M, Z to Broad Street
Bus: M1 M12, M15

Opened in 1994, the George Gustav Heye Center of the
National Museum of the American Indian is located at the historic Alexander Hamilton U.S. Custom House in Lower
Manhattan. The beautiful Beaux Arts building, completed in
1907, is a historic landmark designed by Cass Gilbert. The vast
seven-story structure, with its 450,000 square feet, covers three
city blocks. On the building's huge entrance pedestals are four
large seated female figures representing America, Asia, Europe
and Africa created by Daniel Chester French, who also created
the statue of Abraham Lincoln for the Lincoln Memorial in
Washington, D.C. The Heye Center serves as the National
Museum of the American Indian's exhibition and education
facility for New York City. Part of the Smithsonian Institution,
the center provides a rotating exhibition schedule as well as a
wide range of public programs that explore the diversity of the
Native people of the Americas and the strength and continuity
of their cultures from the earliest times to the present. Programs
offered include music and dance performances, films, and sym-

posia. There is also a resource center and a film and video center accessible to visitors. For updated information on exhibitions and programs, please contact the museum.

Highlights:
Elliptical rotunda and its 140-ton skylight
Reginald Marsh's murals for the rotunda dome

National Sports Museum/Attraction

25 Broadway at Bowling Green (Map 1)

212-837-7950

www.thesportsmuseum.com

Open: Spring 2008. Please check Web site for information.

Subway: 2, 3 to Wall Street; 4, 5 to Bowling Green; R, W to Whitehall/South Ferry.

The National Sports Museum will be opening in Spring 2008 at Bowling Green/the "Canyon of Heroes," in Lower Manhattan. The National Sports Museum/Attraction will be a dynamic and interactive venue dedicated to the history and cultural significance of sports. The first museum of its kind that celebrates all sports, it will offer exhibits and events that feature a variety of sports, teams, players, coaches, cities, and fans. It will also be the home of the Heisman Trophy and the first ever women's hall of fame, the Billie Jean King Women's Sports Hall of Fame. The museum will offer special exhibits as well as a retail shop, a café, and special events spaces. Please check the Web site for updates.

Neue Galerie New York

1048 Fifth Avenue at 86th Street (Map 2)

212-628-6200

www.neuegalerie.org

Open: Sa–M, 11:00 AM–6:00 PM; F, 11:00 AM–9:00 PM. Closed
Tuesday, Wednesday, Thursday, and major holidays

Admission: Adults, $10.00; Seniors and Students, $7.00; Children under
16 must be accompanied by an adult; Children under 12 not admitted

Subway: 4, 5, 6 to 86th Street

Bus: M1, M2, M3, M4 to 86th Street

Opened in the fall of 2001, Neue Galerie New York is a museum dedicated to early twentieth-century German and Austrian
art and design. It was developed by two men who shared a close
friendship for nearly 30 years: art dealer and museum exhibition
organizer Serge Sabarsky and businessman, philanthropist, and art
collector Ronald S. Lauder. Both men shared a passionate com-
mitment to the German and Austrian art of this period and
dreamed of opening a museum to showcase the finest examples
of this work. Located on Fifth Avenue's Museum Mile, Neue
Galerie New York has made its home in the beautiful Carrère &
Hastings building at Fifth Avenue and 86th Street that was once
the home of Mrs. Cornelius Vanderbilt III. The second-floor
galleries are dedicated to art from Vienna circa 1900 and feature
examples of fine art by Gustav Klimt, Egon Schiele, Oskar
Kokoschka, and artists of the Wiener Werkstätte. The third-
floor galleries feature German art representing various movements of the early twentieth century such as the Brücke (Erich
Heckel, Ernst Ludwig Kirchner, Karl Schmidt-Rottluff); the
Blaue Reiter (Vassily Kandinsky, Paul Klee, August Macke);

Neue Sachlichkeit (Otto Dix, George Grosz, Christian Schad) and the Bauhaus (Lyonel Feininger, Oskar Schlemmer). Neue Galerie also launches several temporary exhibitions throughout the year, highlighting German and Austrian art and design.

Highlights
Egon Scheile's *Self-portrait in Brown Coat*
Gustav Klimt's *The Dancer*
Max Beckmann's *Self-portrait with Horn*
Erich Heckel's *Girl with Doll (Fränzi)*

New York City Fire Museum

278 Spring Street (Between Varick and Hudson Street; Map 1)

212-691-1303

www.nycfiremuseum.org

Open: Tu–Sa, 10:00 AM–5:00 PM; Su, 10:00 AM–4:00 PM; Closed
Mondays and major holidays

Admission: Adults, $5.00; Students and Seniors, $2.00; Children under
12, $1.00

Subway: 1, 9 to Houston Street; C, E to Spring Street

Located in a renovated 1904 firehouse in Soho, the New York
City Fire Museum houses one of the nation's most important collections of fire-related art and artifacts from the late eighteenth
century to the present. A walk through the museum takes you
through the history of firefighting, illustrating what firefighting was
like at different times in history since the Colonial period. Among
the treasures found here are the Farnam-style engine, one of the
oldest fire engines in North America, dating back to 1790, and the
horse-drawn 1901 La France steam engine. Along with the engines
are excellent examples of four-wheel hose reels that were once
used in New York City. Also on display is a wide range of firefighting equipment including rescue gear, helmets, lanterns, tools,
and early breathing equipment. Besides the apparatus, the museum
exhibits a large number of other fire service accessories such as
leather fire buckets, painted parade hats, uniform parts, and insignia
and decorative elements from equipment. On the first floor is a
permanent exhibit honoring the 343 firefighters lost in the World
Trade Center on September 11, 2001, that includes a photographic
display as well as artifacts from the site.

New York City Police Museum

100 Old Slip (Between Water Street and South Street, Map 1)
212-480-3100
www.nycpolicemuseum.org

Open: Tu–Sa, 10:00 AM–5:00 PM; Su, 11:00 AM–5:00 PM
Admission: Suggested donation, Adults, $5.00; Seniors, $3.00; Children,
$2.00; Children under 6, Free
Subway: 2, 3 to Wall Street; 4, 5 to Bowling Green; N, R to Whitehall,
South Ferry.

Entertaining exhibits and videos detail the highs and lows of
being a New York City police officer during the past 160 years.
Visitors hear first-person stories about every facet of police life in
the city—from the mounted unit, the vice squad, hostage negoti-
ations, and detective work to the evolution and empowerment of
women on the force. Pose for a police line-up photo, step into an
old-time jail cell, see turn-of-the-century mug shots, and check
out weapons used by the original gangs of New York. On display are photographs and memorabilia chronicling police work
over the years, including uniforms, badges, medals, and vehicles.
The New York City Police Museum gives us a look at life on
both sides of the law—the thugs that threaten us and the brave
that protect us. The Hall of Heroes displays the badges of every
officer killed in the line of duty since 1854, a reminder of the
courage and dedication required to be one of New York's finest.

New York Hall of Science

47-01 111th Street (Map 3)
Located in Flushing Meadows Corona Park
Queens
718-699-0005
www.nyscience.org

Open: M–Th, 9:30 AM–2:00 PM; F, 9:30 AM–5:00 PM (free from
2:00–5:00 PM); Sa & Su, 10:00 AM–6:00 PM (free Su, 10:00–11:00
AM). Free hours suspended during July and August. Closed Labor Day
and Christmas Day
Admission: Adults, $11.00; Seniors, Students, and Children 2–17,
$8.00. Science Playground fee: $3.00 per person, $2.00 for groups plus
general hall admission fee
Subway: 7 train to 111th Street. Walk 3 blocks south
Bus: Q23 or Q53 to Corona Avenue and 108th Street

The New York Hall of Science is ranked one of America's best
science museums and is New York City's only museum dedicated to hands-on, interactive science and technology exhibitions
and education. Wander underneath the 35-foot glucose molecule
that hovers over Exhibition Hall and explore the microscopic
world of molecules. Surf the Web at the Technology Gallery or
discover the science of living things in the new Pfizer Foundation
Biochemistry Discovery Lab—the first hands-on lab in the
world that is open to the public and devoted entirely to biochemistry. Recently expanded with a 55,000-square-foot addition, some of the new exhibits include Preschool Place for children under the age of 6 where they can learn and explore in the
natural and built world of a city, find the ways in which urban
and natural landscapes are interrelated with different activities,

play in the multi-ethnic market, move bricks on a conveyor system, and make believe in a two-story cityscape. Also included is a multisensory activity area for babies 18 months and younger. The Sports Challenge allows visitors to ride a wave on a surfboard or climb a rock wall while learning about the science behind the sport. Each exhibit focuses on a different scientific principle that is crucial to succeeding at that particular sport. The 5,000-square-foot redesigned Rocket Park chronicles, in words and pictures, the history of the U.S. space program. Those are just a few of the things to discover at the New York Hall of Science where visitors are encouraged to explore and experiment and learn about the physics, chemistry, and biology behind everyday life.

The New-York Historical Society

170 Central Park West at 77th Street (Map 2)
212-873-3400
www.nyhistory.org

Open: Museum, Tu–Su, 10:00–6:00 PM. Closed Mondays. Library,
Tu–Sa, 10:00 AM–5:00 PM. Closed Mondays and Tuesdays
Admissions: Adults, $10.00; Seniors, Students, and Teachers, $5.00;
Children under 12 accompanied by an adult, Free. Library access is free
Subway: B, C to 81st Street; 1, 9 to 79th Street

The New-York Historical Society was started in 1804 and is
home to one of the nation's most distinguished independent
research libraries and New York City's oldest museum. The second historical society established in the country, it was created
with the foresight of its founders to preserve the history of a city
and country then in its infancy. The society's collection includes
more than 4.5 million American history-related documents,
paintings, artifacts, and ephemera. A large part of the permanent
collection is housed in the Henry Luce III Center for the Study
of American Culture and offers visitors access to nearly 40,000
museum objects like George Washington's camp bed at Valley
Forge and a collection of more than 550 American board games
from the Civil War to the present. Its art holdings comprise
more than 1.6 million works, among them a world-class collection of Hudson River School paintings and a sculpture collection of over 800 works from the colonial period to the present.
The furniture collection contains over 500 pieces, including
chairs from Napoleon and Louis XVI and the desk at which
Clement Clarke Moore wrote "A Visit from St. Nicholas."
Decorative arts, tools for home and trade, and a number of small

collections, including badges, jewelry, textiles, military gear, souvenirs, and toys are also on display. The reference library, which is open to the public free of charge, houses general collections and includes all materials not held in the manuscript department or the department of prints, photographs, and architectural collections. It contains books and pamphlets, newspapers, magazines and journals, broadsides, hotel files, maps, menus, and sheet music. The society launches several temporary exhibitions each year. Slavery and the Making of New York, a two-year initiative opening in October 2005, draws on the society's exceptional collection of materials documenting slavery and reconstruction.

Additional Highlights:

John James Audubon's original preparatory watercolors for *The Birds of America*

Tiffany Lamp Collection

Lumen Reed Portrait Gallery which explores the history of art collecting in New York City throughout the nineteenth century

The New York Public Library

Fifth Avenue at 42nd Street (Map 2)
212-661-7220
www.nypl.org

Open: Tu–W, 11:00 AM–7:30 PM; Th–Sa, 10:00 AM–6:00 PM; Su, 1:00
PM–6:00 PM
Admission: Free
Subway: 4, 5, 6 to 42nd Street/Grand Central; B, D, F to 42nd Street
Bus: M1, M2, M3, M4, M5, M42, M104 to Fifth Avenue and 42nd Street

The New York Public Library is considered one of the great
knowledge institutions in the world whose collections rank with
those of the British Library, the Library of Congress, and the
Bibliothèque National de France. Virtually all of the library's
many collections and services are freely available to visitors.
Chartered in 1895, the NYPL was created by the Astor and
Lenox Libraries and the Samuel Tilden Trust with the mission of
making knowledge accessible and free to the public. The main
building, NYPL's beautiful Carrère & Hastings Beaux Arts
building, houses the Humanities and Social Sciences Library —
one of the four research libraries within the NYPL system. It is
also home to Patience and Fortitude, the famous lions that stand
guard at the entrance to the building. Approximately 12 to 15
exhibitions are launched each year at this site, drawing on the
strength of its collections. Past exhibitions have included
Drawings by Charles Addams, Depression-era Prints and
Photographs from the WPA and FSA, Liturgical Manuscripts,
Herman Melville's *Moby Dick*, Celebrity Caricature in America,
and The Romanovs: Their Empire, Their Books. For up-to-date
schedules and information, please call or check the Web site.

The New York Public Library for the Performing Arts

Dorothy and Lewis B. Cullman Center (Map 2)

40 Lincoln Center Plaza (Between the Metropolitan Opera House and the Vivian Beaumont Theater)

111 Amsterdam Avenue (entrance at 65th Street)

212-870-1630

www.nypl.org

Open: Tu, W, F, Sa, Noon–6:00 PM; Th, Noon–8:00 PM

Admission: Free

Subway: 1, 9 to 66th Street; A, C or B, D to 59th Street Columbus Circle

The New York Public Library for the Performing Arts houses one of the world's most extensive combinations of circulating, reference, and rare archival collections in its field. As one of NYPL's special research libraries, the Performing Arts Library is particularly well known for its prodigious collections of nonbook materials such as historic recordings, videotapes, autograph materials, correspondence, sheet music, stage designs, press clippings, programs, posters, and photographs. Drawing on the vast holdings, the library launches several temporary exhibitions throughout the year. Past exhibitions have included The Enduring Legacy of George Balanchine; Centennial Salute to Al Hirschfeld; Best of Times: The Theatre of Charles Dickens; and Pink Cadillacs and Yellow Submarines: Transportation in a Century of Popular Music Recordings. For up-to-date schedules and information on exhibitions, please call or check the Web site.

New York Transit Museum

Corner of Boerum Place & Schermerhorn Street (Map 4)
Brooklyn Heights
718-694-1600
www.mta.info/museum

Open: Tu–F, 10:00 AM–4:00 PM; Sa & Su, Noon–5:00 PM. Closed
Mondays and holidays
Admission: $5.00; Seniors and Children 3-17, $3.00
Subway: 2, 3, 4, 5* to Borough Hall; M, N, R to Court Street; A, C, G to
Hoyt-Schermerhorn Street; A, C, F to Jay Street/Borough Hall
*Weekdays during rush hour only

Housed in a historic 1936 subway station in Brooklyn Heights,
the New York Transit Museum is the largest museum in the
United States devoted to urban public transportation history.
The museum explores the development of the New York
Metropolitan area through the presentation of exhibitions, tours,
educational programs, and workshops dealing with the cultural,
social, and technological history of public transportation. The
museum's refurbished galleries feature popular exhibits such as
Steel, Stone, and Backbone, which recounts the tale of building
New York City's 100-year old subway system featuring photographs taken over 100 years ago during construction and includes
historical artifacts and videos. The On the Streets Gallery contains several interactive exhibits that provide an in-depth look at
New York City's trolleys and buses. It presents a history of
above-ground mobility for the last 176 years—from the early
1800s through the twenty-first century. Central to this exhibition
is a simulated traffic intersection complete with traffic lights,
parking meters, fire hydrants, and coordinating walk/don't walk

signs. Other items include a refurbished 1960s bus cab and a child-size trolley. The New York Transit Museum Gallery Annex & Store is located in Grand Central Terminal and features transportation-themed revolving exhibits in their gallery space.

Highlights:
The Dr. George T. F. Rahilly Trolley and Bus Study Center featuring over 50 detailed models of trolleys and work cars

Nicholas Roerich Museum

319 West 107th Street (Map 2)
212-864-7752
www.roerich.org

Open: Tu–Su, 2:00 PM–5:00 PM. Closed Mondays
Admission: Free
Subway: 1 to 110th Street
Bus: M104 to 108th Street/Broadway

The Nicholas Roerich Museum is a major center for the exhibition of paintings by Russian-born Nicholas Roerich and makes available to the public reproductions of his art and numerous books about his life and work. The museum's aim is to promote Roerich's ideas about art and culture which are embodied in the Museum's symbol and motto, *Pax Cultura*: Peace through Culture. It was Roerich's belief that the role of cultural development in the peace and evolution of the world is fundamental and that it is therefore the responsibility of those who work in creative and cultural fields to always strive for that peace and evolution. Their work, he believed, should always be guided by those impulses. Roerich created thousands of paintings during his lifetime, and the museum displays approximately 200 that are permanently on view. His paintings explore the mythic origins, the natural beauty, and the spiritual strivings of humanity and of the world. The museum also maintains an active schedule of chamber music concerts.

The Noble Maritime Collection

Snug Harbor Cultural Center (Map 4)
1000 Richmond Terrace, Building D
Staten Island
718-447-6490
www.noblemaritime.org
Open: Th–Su, 1:00 PM–5:00 PM. Closed New Year's Day, Easter,
Independence Day, Thanksgiving Day, and Christmas Day
Admission: Adults, $3.00; Seniors, Students, and Educators, $2.00;
Children under 10, Free
Directions: From the Staten Island Ferry terminal, take the S40 bus to
the front of the site

Located on the grounds of Snug Harbor Cultural Center, The
Noble Maritime Collection is one of the country's most significant maritime collections and serves as a catalyst for the preservation of art and study of maritime history. Born in Paris is 1913,
John Noble was the son of the noted American artist, John
"Wichita Bill" Noble and spent his early years in the studios of
his father and his father's contemporaries — artists and writers of
the early part of the 20th century. The family moved to the
United States in 1919 ("the greatest wooden ship launching year
in the history of the world") when Noble's fascination with ships
began. This led to a career as a seaman on schooners and in
marine salvage for nearly 20 years, and in 1941, Noble began to
build his floating studio out of parts of vessels he salvaged. From
1946 on, Noble worked as a full-time artist. The collection
includes John Noble's Houseboat Studio, the restored houseboat
where Noble created paintings, drawings, and lithographs for
over 40 years and where Noble chronicled twentieth-century
working ships and the New York Harbor. In The Writing
Room, photographs, paintings, etchings, furnishings, and unusual

ship models provide the visitor with an early history of Sailors' Snug Harbor, the former retirement home for mariners, and see a recreated mariners' room circa 1900 as it might have looked in a part of the museum that was once a dormitory. Furniture, bed linens, and chairs show how the retired seamen lived in Sailors' Snug Harbor, the oldest charitable institution in America. Galleries are constantly changing to feature local artists and education programs are offered throughout the year.

The Noguchi Museum

32-37 Vernon Boulevard (Map 3)
Long Island City, Queens
718-204-7088
www.noguchi.org

Open: W–F, 10:00 AM–5:00 PM; Sa & Su, 11:00–6:00 PM. Closed
Mondays & Tuesdays
Admission: Adults, $5.00; Students and Seniors, $2.50
Subway: N, W to Broadway stop in Queens. Walk ten blocks down
Broadway toward the East River and the Manhattan skyline. Broadway
ends and turns into Vernon Boulevard. On the weekends, there is a shut-
tle bus service that goes between the Asia Society at Park Avenue and
70th Street and the Noguchi Museum. Buses leave the front of the Asia
Society at 12:30, 1:30, 2:30, 3:30 PM and leave from the front of the
Noguchi Museum every hour on the hour from 1:00 PM until 6:00 PM.
The fare is $5.00 one-way and $10.00 round-trip. Museum admission is
not included.

Created by Isamu Noguchi, The Noguchi Museum opened in
1985 to display a comprehensive collection of the famed sculptor's
artwork in a peaceful setting created by the artist. The collection—works in stone, wood, clay, and metal; models for public
projects and gardens; dance sets; and Noguchi's Akari Light
Sculptures—is housed in thirteen galleries within a converted
factory building that encircles a garden containing granite and
basalt sculptures. A recent renovation added an education center,
a new café, a shop, and a heating and cooling system to allow the
museum to remain open all year long. A recently launched program of temporary exhibits will be followed by the creation of a
special gallery devoted to Noguchi's work in interior design.

Old Stone House

J.J. Byrne Park (Map 4)
Third Street between 4th & 5th Avenues
Brooklyn
718-768-3195

Open: Sa & Su, 11:00 AM–4:00 PM
Admission: Suggested donation, $3.00; Children under 12, Free
Subway: F, R, N local to 4th Avenue/9th Street

The Old Stone House in the Park Slope/Gowanus neighborhood in Brooklyn is now a Historic Interpretive Center in J. J. Byrne Park. Built in 1699 beside the Gowanus Creek, the house later played a role in the Battle of Brooklyn on August 27, 1776. Strategically positioned, the house was occupied by the British and turned into an artillery position to fire upon defeated American soldiers. The house was held by an estimated 2,000 British and hired Hessian soldiers and against this stronghold some 400 of the Maryland Brigade threw themselves into several attacks, ultimately being defeated but allowing George Washington and his troops to escape. In the 1890s, the house served as the first clubhouse of the Brooklyn team of the National Baseball League, later known as the Brooklyn Dodgers. The house had been demolished, and in the 1930s it was rebuilt with the original stones to serve as a sports facility in the newly opened J. J. Byrne Park. After two more restorations in the 1970s and the 1990s, the house is again open to the public. This replica of the original house is home to an educational center offering an exhibit about the Battle of Brooklyn, tours, education programs, public programs, and special events.

P. S. 1 Contemporary Art Center

22-25 Jackson Avenue at 46th Avenue (Map 3)

Long Island City, Queens

718-784-2084

www.ps1.org

Open: Th–M, Noon–6:00 PM. Closed Tuesdays & Wednesdays

Admission: Suggested donation, Adults, $5.00; Seniors and Students, $2.00

Subway: 7 to 45th Road/Courthouse Square; E, V* to 23rd Street/Ely Avenue; G to 21st Street/Van Alst or Court Street.

*V does not run on weekends

Bus: Q67 to Jackson and 46th Avenue; B61 to 46th Avenue

P. S. 1 Contemporary Art Center, an affiliate of The Museum of Modern Art, is the oldest and second largest nonprofit arts center in the United States solely devoted to contemporary art. P. S. 1 was founded in 1971 by Alanna Heiss as The Institute of Art and Urban Resources, Inc., and was primarily dedicated to the transformation of abandoned and underutilized buildings in New York City into exhibition, performance, and studio spaces for artists. Housed in an old public school building, P. S. 1 stands out from major art institutions through its cutting-edge approach to exhibitions and its direct involvement with artists. While there is no permanent collection aside from approximately 15 works of art commissioned for the opening of the Center, P. S. 1 launches rotating exhibitions at the center as well as at its other location, the Clocktower Gallery in Manhattan.

Poe Cottage

Poe Park (Map 3)
East Kingsbridge Road and the Grand Concourse
Bronx
718-881-8900
www.bronxhistoricalsociety.org

Open: Sa, 10:00 AM–4:00 PM; Su, 1:00 PM–5:00 PM. Groups can be scheduled for visits during the week
Admission: Adults, $3.00; Seniors, Students, and Children, $2.00
Subway: 4, D to Kingsbridge Road

The tiny Poe Cottage was the last home of great American poet, Edgar Allan Poe (1809–1849). With hopes that a move to the country would help his wife's condition (she suffered from tuberculosis), Poe, his wife, Virginia, and her mother moved into the cottage that they leased for $100 a year. Set in a small park on the Grand Concourse in the Bronx, Poe Cottage is the only house left from the old village of Fordham. Built in 1812, this one-and-a-half-story cottage was typical of the workmen's houses that were found in the Bronx. Though Poe achieved literary success, he was penniless due to a bad business venture, and it was during this bleak time that Poe wrote some of his most memorable poems like "Annabel Lee" and "The Bells." The cottage contains a sparsely furnished main floor with items that include a nineteenth-century cast-iron stove, a desk, a rocking chair, a straw bed, and a mirror that may have been used by Poe. A narrow staircase leads up to the couple's attic bedroom. On display are painted and sculpted portraits of the author, as well as early photographs and drawings of the cottage. There is an audiovisual show that detail's Poe's life in Fordham and his creative pursuits.

Prospect Park Audubon Center

Prospect Park near Ocean Avenue/Lincoln Road entrance (Map 4)
Brooklyn
718-287-3400
www.prospectpark.org

Open: Spring & fall: Th–Su, Noon–5:00 PM; summer: Th–Su, Noon–6:00 PM; winter: Sa & Su, Noon–4:00 PM
Admission: Free. Electric boat tour costs $5.00 for adults and $3.00 for Seniors and Children
Subway: Q, S, B to Prospect Park
Bus: B16, B41, B43, B48

The first urban-area Audubon Center in the nation, the Prospect Park Audubon Center is a place of active discovery with hands-on exhibits and innovative programming for children and adults. Exhibits allow visitors to explore a world of nature through interactive technology and acres of restored natural habitat just outside. The center is located in the park's 1905 Beaux Arts Boathouse, a recently renovated historic landmark whose design was inspired by a famous sixteenth-century Venetian library. Overlooking the park's serene Lullwater, the Audubon Center also features tours on the electric boat *Independence*, a replica of a boat used in the park over 100 years ago. A staff of Audubon naturalists lead free bird-watching tours and nature walks every weekend. The Audubon Center also houses the Prospect Park Visitors Center and the Songbird Café & Giftshop, where visitors can pick up field guides, nature-inspired toys and novelties, and park gear. Annual events like the Earth Day Celebration and Hawk Weekend attract thousands for live bird shows, performances, nature workshops, and more.

Queens County Farm Museum

73-50 Little Neck Parkway (Map 3)
Floral Park, Queens
718-347-3276
www.queensfarm.org

Open: Year-round, M–Fr, 9:00 AM–5:00 PM (outdoor visiting only); Sa &
Su, 10:00 AM–5:00 PM when tours of the historic farmhouse and
hayrides are available (April–November, weather permitting)
Admission: Free except for special events and group tours

The Queens County Farmhouse Museum occupies New York
City's largest remaining tract of undisturbed farmland and is the
largest working historical farm in the City. The farm encompasses
a 47-acre parcel of land that is the longest continuously farmed
site in New York State. It includes historic farm buildings, a
greenhouse complex, livestock, farm vehicles and tools, planting
fields, an orchard and an herb garden; and in 2004, a vineyard
was planted. The museum offers a diverse range of special events
throughout the year, including pumpkin picking, Apple Fest, a
county fair and an interactive corn maze in the fall, Farm Fest in
spring, and an American Indian Pow Wow in summer.

Queens Museum of Art

New York City Building (Map 3
Flushing Meadows Corona Park
Queens
718-592-9700
www.queensmuseum.org

Open: W–F, 10:00 AM–5:00 PM; Sa & Su, Noon–5:00 PM
Admission: Suggested donation for Adults, $5.00; Seniors and Students,
$2.50; Children under 5, Free
Subway: 7 train to Willet Point/Shea Stadium. Bus: Q48 to Roosevelt
Avenue and 111th Street; Q23, Q58 to Corona Avenue and 51st Avenue

Founded in 1972 to provide a cultural center to the country's
most ethnically diverse county, the Queens Museum of Art
continues to serve the varied communities through temporary
exhibitions of contemporary art and broader subjects relating to
the culture of the borough and the historic site on which the
museum stands. Housed in the New York City Building that
was built for the 1939 World's Fair, it is the only surviving structure from that event. In the years following the Second World
War, the building served as the home to the General Assembly
of the United Nations until 1951 before returning to its original
purpose as a pavilion for the 1964 World's Fair. It housed the
Panorama of the City of New York, still the museum's most
popular attraction, and the museum continues to acknowledge
the site's rich history through its programming. On permanent
display are exhibitions about the 1939 and 1964 World's Fairs with
over 6,000 objects, including memorabilia, photography, audio
tape, video, and 8mm and 16mm film. Another QMA permanent exhibition is Tiffany by Design: Selections from the

Neustadt Museum Collection, which contains lamps, windows, and glass designed by Louis Comfort Tiffany. The Queens Museum of Art is the principle fine arts collecting institution in Queens and also launches a wide variety of temporary exhibits and public programs.

Highlight:
The panorama of the City of New York

Rose Museum at Carnegie Hall

154 West 57th Street at 7th Avenue (Map 2)

2nd Floor

212-903-9629

www.carnegiehall.org

Open: Daily, 11:00 AM–4:30 PM and to concertgoers in the evening

Admission: Free

Subway: N, R, Q to 7th Avenue/57th Street; 1, 9 to Columbus Circle

From the collection of the Carnegie Hall Archive, 300 objects are on display at the Rose Museum at any one time for visitors to discover and marvel at. The collection process started in 1986 in anticipation of the centennial anniversary of Carnegie Hall in 1991; and with the donation of Bennie Goodman's clarinet and funding from Susan and Elihu Rose, a museum to honor this institution was born. The museum quickly acquired an impressive collection from donations, searches, and purchases from thousands of people worldwide. The museum opened in time for the centennial with an exhibit of Tchaikovsky that opened 100 years to the day that Tchaikovsky opened the hall. From the silver trowel that Mrs. Carnegie used to lay the cornerstone to architectural drawings of the hall to live recordings, a visitor is invited to experience some of the treasures that have made Carnegie Hall legendary. Exhibits from the permanent collection rotate from time to time, and temporary exhibitions are launched on a regular basis in conjunction with events on stage and major anniversaries. Previous exhibitions have included Leonard Bernstein's fiftieth anniversary of his 1943 debut, the centennial of George and Ira Gershwin, Marian Anderson's one hundredth birthday and Schubert's two hundredth anniversary. Most of the exhibition materials used were never before seen by the public.

Rubin Museum of Art

150 West 17th Street (east of 7th Avenue; Map 1)

212-620-5000

www.rmanyc.org

Open: Tu, Sa, 11:00 AM–7:00 PM; W, Su, 11:00 AM–5:00 PM; Th, F, 11:00 AM–9:00 PM. Closed Mondays

Admission: Adults, $7.00; Seniors, Students, Artists, and Neighbors (in zipcodes 10011 & 10001), $5.00; Children 11 and under, Free

Subway: 1, 9 to 18th Street/7th Avenue

Opened in October of 2004, the Rubin Museum of Art is home to one of the most comprehensive collections of Himalayan art in the world. RMA's collection consists of paintings, sculptures, and textiles that range in date over two millennia, though most works of art in the collection reflect major periods and schools of Himalayan art from the twelfth century forward. The exhibitions are organized with great care to assist visitors who are new to Himalayan art. Wall texts and interpretive panels provide aesthetic, social, and historical perspectives to both scholars and the average viewer. The ExploreArt Galleries on the third, fifth and sixth floors take the viewer behind the scenes, answering questions about why and for whom the art was made. Exhibitions are drawn from the approximately 1,200 objects in the permanent collection and are augmented by periodic loan exhibitions to further explore the diversity and cultural heritage of Himalayan art.

Schomburg Center for Research in Black Culture

515 Malcolm X Boulevard (Map 3)

212-491-2200

www.nypl.org

Open: Tu–Sa, 10:00 AM–6:00 PM; Su, 1:00 PM–5:00 PM. Closed Mondays

Admission: Free

Subway: 2, 3 to 135th Street

Bus: M7, M102

One of the four research libraries within the New York Public Library system, the Schomburg Center for Research in Black Culture is a national research center dedicated to collecting, preserving, and providing access to resources documenting the experiences of peoples of African descent throughout the world. Dedicated to making knowledge accessible and free to the public, the New York Public Library's Schomburg Center presents temporary exhibitions throughout the year drawing upon their vast collection. Past exhibitions have included Romare Bearden: From the Studio and Archive, The James Baldwin Series, Blacks and the U.S. Constitution, The Art of African American Women: Empowering Traditions, and Black New York Photographers of the twentieth Century. For up-to-date information on exhibitions, please call or check the Web site.

The Skyscraper Museum

39 Battery Place on the Ground floor of the Ritz Carlton Hotel (Map 1)

212-968-1961

www.skyscraper.org

Open: W–Su, Noon–6:00 PM. Closed Mondays & Tuesdays

Admission: Adults, $5.00; Seniors and Students, $2.50

Subway: 4, 5 to Bowling Green; 1, 9, R, W to Rector Street; J, V to Broad Street

The Skyscraper Museum, now in its dazzling modern gallery in Battery Park City, is devoted to the study of high-rise building past, present, and future and celebrates and explores the role of the skyscraper in shaping the identity of the city. The museum's interior features a polished stainless steel floor and ceiling that create the illusion of a towering multilevel space. Special exhibits explore tall buildings as objects of design, products of technology, and places to work and live. The museum is also committed to collecting and preserving important artifacts of high-rise history and has an active education program (education@skyscraper.org). The museum's gift shop features exciting items, toys, and books about skyscrapers and architecture. The interactive Web site is expansive and up to date and offers further insight into the museum's current exhibits as well as its archive, special projects, and programs.

Solomon R. Guggenheim Museum

1071 Fifth Avenue at 89th Street (Map 2)
212-423-3500
www.guggenheim.org

Open: Sa–W, 10:00 AM–5:45 PM; F, 10:00 AM–8:00 PM. Closed
Thursdays and Christmas Day
Admission: Adults, $15.00; Seniors and Students, $10.00; Children
under 12, Free.
Subway: 4, 5, 6 to 86th Street and walk west to Fifth Avenue and north
to 88th Street

Housed in the world-renowned building designed by Frank
Lloyd Wright, the Guggenheim is home to a vast collection of
modern and contemporary painting and sculpture. The building
itself—recalling the spiral structure of a chambered nautilus—
offers visitors a unique experience in which to view the impressive collection from top to bottom with natural light illuminating
each of the six levels. The ten-story tower, added in 1992, allows
for larger installations and enables the museum to display more of
its 10,000-piece permanent collection. Originally established in
1939 by Solomon R. Guggenheim and his artist-friend and advi-
sor Hilla Rebay as a home for avant-garde art, the Guggenheim
collection has grown to incorporate a wide variety of notable
artists. Home to one of the largest collections of Kandinsky
paintings in the world, other masters represented include
Brancusi, Chagall, Delaunay, Klee, Lichtenstein, Modigliani,
Picasso, Pissarro, Pollock, Renoir and van Gogh.

Sony Wonder Technology Lab

56th Street between Madison and Fifth Avenue (Map 2)

212-833-8100

www.sonywondertechlab.com

Open: Tu–Sa, 10:00 AM–5:00 PM; Su, Noon–5:00 PM. Closed Mondays and major holidays

Admission: Free. Reservations are strongly recommended and can be made Tu–F, 8:00 AM–2:00 PM at 212-833-5414

Subway: 4, 5, 6 to 59th Street; E, F to 53rd Street; N, R to 60th Street

Located at Sony Plaza in midtown Manhattan, visitors are welcome to explore the world of entertainment and technology at Sony Wonder Technology Lab, a four-floor interactive environment featuring the latest in technology and digital entertainment. Start at Log In where you personalize your exhibit card to access and document your visit and move on to the Communication Bridge where a timeline of over 150 years of communication technology and media history reminds of us of how things used to work and how far we've come. Move on to one-of-a-kind exhibits like the Audio Lab, where you can digitally place sound effects into music or the Television Production Studio where you can participate in a simulated production of a television show. Other state-of-the-art exhibits include Medical Imaging where you can take a look inside the human body to diagnose and treat a variety of ailments and Wonder of Games that explores the history and development of computer and video games. No matter what your interest or age, there is something for everyone at this emporium to entertainment technology.

South Street Seaport Museum

12 Fulton Street (between Front and South Street; Map 1)
212-748-8600
www.southstseaport.org

Open: Winter (from Nov 1) F–M, 10:00 AM–5:00 PM;summer (from Apr 1), Tu–Su, 10:00 AM–6:00 PM
Admission: Adults, $8.00; Seniors and Students, $6.00; Children Age 5–12, $4.00; Children under 5, Free
Subway: 2, 3, 4, 5, J, Z, M to Fulton Street; A, C to Broadway-Nassau

The South Street Seaport Museum is located on the site that was once the country's leading port and is now a 12-square-block historic district on the East River in Lower Manhattan. The area features historic buildings, various shops, the Fulton Fish Market (due to move to the South Bronx), and historic ships tied up at the East River. The museum mounts exhibitions in restored buildings and on historic ships, drawing on a collection of paintings, photographs, models, and tools relating to shipbuilding, maritime history, and the neighboring historic district. Home to one of the largest collections of historic vessels in the world, three are open for public visitation — *Wavertree*, a full-rigged ship, *Peking*, a four-masted barque, and *Ambrose*, an ocean lightship — and two schooners are used for public sails and charters. Part of the museum's working collection, Bowne & Co., Stationers at 211 Water Street is a recreation of a nineteenth-century printing shop. Staff use antique printing presses and a large collection of nineteenth-century typefaces to create greeting cards, invitations, and other printed materials. The museum also offers living history programs, special events, and educational programs for children and adults.

Staten Island Children's Museum

Snug Harbor Cultural Center (Map 4)
1000 Richmond Terrace
Staten Island

718-273-2060

Open: Summer, Tu–Su, 11:00 AM–5:00 PM; winter hours, Tu–Su, Noon–5:00 PM. Closed Mondays and Thanksgiving Day and Christmas Day

Admission: General, $5.00; Children under 1, Free

Directions: From the Staten Island Ferry terminal, take the S40 bus (Richmond Terrace) to Snug Harbor

Located at Snug Harbor Cultural Center, the Staten Island Children's Museum is more like a playground where children can explore and learn, in a creative environment, about the world in which we live. Sail a pirate ship and cook in the galley at Block Harbor, explore a rainforest canopy or drive a dogsled at Great Explorations, or crawl through an ant home, watch butterflies being born, and visit the Arthropod Zoo at Bugs and Other Insects. These are just a handful of fun and exciting things that await children at the Staten Island Children's Museum. Daily events include Feeding Time, where visitors can watch, learn, and assist while museum curators feed and care for bugs, fish, guinea pigs, and Kimba, the museum's pet bird (a sun conure) and Story Time, where fables, tales, and stories from around the world are told. The museum also offers a number of special events and activities for children and adults alike. Call for information on upcoming programs, "free days," and extended hours.

Staten Island Historical Society

441 Clarke Avenue (Map 4)
Staten Island
/18-351-1611
www.historicrichmondtown.org

The Staten Island Historical Society is located at Historic
Richmond Town and together with the City of New York
through the Department of Cultural Affairs, it oversees operations and the various programs and events that are offered there
throughout the year. The historical society also maintains a
research library and archive that is open by appointment only.
For additional information, please see the separate entry for
Historic Richmond Town.

The Studio Museum in Harlem

144 West 125th Street between Lenox Avenue & Seventh Avenue (Map 3)
212-864-4500
www.studiomuseum.org

Open: W–F, Noon–6:00 PM; Sa, 10:00 AM–6:00 PM; Su, Noon–6:00
PM; Closed Mondays & Tuesdays and major holidays
Admission: Suggested donation for Adults, $7.00; Seniors and Students,
$3.00; Children under 12, Free.
Subway: 2, 3, 4, 5, 6, A, B, C, D to 125th Street

The Studio Museum in Harlem is a contemporary museum that
focuses on the work of artists of African descent from all over
the world as well as work that has been inspired and influenced
by African American culture. Since opening in 1968, the museum has earned recognition for its role in promoting the works of
artists of African descent through its exhibitions, Artists-in-
Residence program, permanent collection, education and public
programming, as well as its archival and research facilities. The
permanent collection includes over 1,600 paintings, sculptures,
watercolors, drawings, pastels, prints, photographs, mixed-media
works, and installations by a number of artists. Some of the
artists represented include Romare Bearden, Melvin Edwards,
Lois Mailou Jones, Norman Lewis, and Betye Saar. The museum also maintains an extensive archive of the work of photographer James VanDerZee, the quintessential chronicler of Harlem
from 1906 to 1983. Currently undergoing a renovation, the museum is expanding the current 60,000-square-foot space to 72,000
square feet, and the new design will provide clear visual access of
the museum with direct views from the street into the museum
lobby, galleries, and the glass-enclosed sculpture garden.

Theodore Roosevelt Birthplace

28 East 20th Street (between Broadway and Park Avenue South; Map 1)
212-260-1616
www.nps.gov/thrb

Open: Tu–Sa, 9:00 AM–5:00 PM. Closed Sundays & Mondays and on all
federal holidays
Admission: $3.00 per person; Children under 16, Free; guided tours on
the hour from 10:00 AM–4:00 PM
Subway: 6, N, R to 23rd Street
Bus: M1, M2, M3, M6, M7 to 20th Street

The original birthplace of Theodore Roosevelt, the twenty-sixth
president of the United States, Roosevelt lived at this site until
the age of 14. He was a sickly child who started an exercise program at the house's outdoor gymnasium, and this led to his life-
long passion for the "strenuous life." This ultimately enabled him
to pursue his boyhood dreams as a rancher, naturalist, explorer,
author, and colonel in the Rough Riders. Roosevelt went on to a
career in political service, including reforming the U.S. Civil
Service Commission and the New York City Police Department
and serving terms as governor of New York and vice president of
the United States. As president he was noted for his progressive
reforms such as preservation of public lands and trust busting and
negotiating an end to the war between Russia and Japan (for
which he won the Nobel Peace Prize). The original house he
lived in was demolished in 1916, and in 1919, shortly after
Roosevelt's death, the Women's Roosevelt Memorial
Association purchased the property and reconstructed the original house, rebuilding and decorating it with most of the original
furnishings. The house contains five period rooms circa 1860 and

two museum galleries that display a variety of artifacts from throughout his lifetime. Among the many items are historical documents, portraits of the Roosevelt family, hunting trophies, his bugle, and the shirt (with bullet hole) that he was wearing the day an assassination attempt was made on his life. A 25-minute film about Roosevelt's childhood is shown upon request.

Additional Highlights:

Roosevelt's Rough Riders uniform

The presidential exercise bicycle

A jar with the first scoop of dirt shoveled out of the Panama Canal site

Ukrainian Museum

222 East 6th Street (between Second & Third Avenues; Map 1)
212-228-0110
www.ukrainianmuseum.org

Open: W–Su, 1:00 PM–5:00 PM. Closed Mondays & Tuesdays
Admission: Adults, $8.00; Seniors and Students, $6.00; Children under 12, Free
Subway: 6 to Astor Place; N, R to Broadway/8th Street; F train to Second Avenue/2nd Street

Open to the public since 1976, the Ukrainian Museum functions to preserve the cultural heritage of Ukrainian immigrants who have settled in the United States and Canada since the turn of the twentieth century. The museum was founded by the Ukrainian National Women's League of America (UNWLA), the largest Ukrainian women's organization in the United States. Part of the mission of this organization emphasized the preservation of the Ukrainian folk culture. The UNWLA mounted an exhibition for the 1933 World's Fair in Chicago that comprised folk costumes, kilims, embroidered and woven textiles, ceramics, and decorative wood objects as well as pysanky, Ukrainian Easter eggs. A large part of this exhibition now serves as the core collection of the Ukrainian Museum. While previously housed in the top two floors of a brownstone, the museum has moved to a much larger and more modern space that can more comfortably display the collection that has grown considerably over the years. While the folk art collection was the seed of the collection, there is a photograph/documentary collection with vintage photographs, films, documents, private correspondence of notable individuals, playbills, and posters; a fine-arts collection of paintings, drawings, woodcuts, etchings, and sculptures and an archival collection with an impressive array of Ukrainian coins, paper money, and stamps. The museum launches two to three exhibits per year from its collections or from loans as well as lectures, conferences, symposiums and gallery talks. Also offered are a variety of traditional Ukrainian folk courses and workshops.

Valentine-Varian House

3266 Bainbridge Avenue (Map 3)

Bronx

718-881-8900

www.bronxhistoricalsociety.org

Open: Sa, 10:00 AM–4:00 PM; Su, 1:00 PM–5:00 PM. Groups by
appointment during the week

Admission: Adults, $3.00; Seniors, Students, and Children, $2.00

Subway: 4 to Mosholu Parkway; D to 205th Street

Built by farmer and blacksmith Isaac Valentine along the ancient
Boston Post Road, it was occupied by both British and
American forces throughout the Revolutionary War. The circa
1758 fieldstone farmhouse is open to the public as the Museum of
Bronx History. Displayed in modern gallery spaces, there are
permanent and changing exhibitions on the history and heritage
of the Bronx and its peoples. The house is owned and operated
by the Bronx County Historical Society and is set on one acre
of gardens that are accessible to visitors.

Van Cortlandt House Museum

Van Cortlandt Park (Map 3)
Broadway at West 246th Street
718-543-3344
www.vancortlandthouse.org

Open: Tu–F, 10:00 AM–3:00 PM; Sa & Su, 11:00 AM–4:00 PM. Closed
Mondays and major holidays
Admission: Adults, $5.00; Seniors and Students, $3.00; Children 12 and
under, Free. Free general admission on Wednesdays
Subway: 1, 9 to 242nd Street
Bus: Bx9 to Broadway/West 246th Street

Van Cortlandt House Museum is New York City's first house
museum, operating since 1897 as a public museum by the
National Society of Colonial Dames in the State of New York.
The mid-eighteenth-century Georgian home was built by
Frederick Van Cortlandt and was the center of an expansive and
prosperous wheat plantation. The interpretive period of the
museum house is from 1748 to 1823, when Frederick and his two
eldest sons, James and Augustus, owned the property. The
museum collection contains Van Cortlandt family materials and
furnishings appropriate to this period. The museum offers hands-
on history school programs and a wide variety of public programs throughout the year.

Highlights
The oldest dollhouse in the country
A Massachusetts kneehole desk
Partial service of Chinese export porcelain

Whitney Museum of American Art

945 Madison Avenue at 75th Street (Map 2)

1-800-WHITNEY; Ticketing, 1-877-WHITNEY

www.whitney.org

Open: W, Th, 11:00 AM–6:00 PM; F, 1:00 PM–9:00 PM; Sa & Su, 11:00
AM–6:00 PM. Closed Mondays & Tuesdays and Thanksgiving Day,
Christmas Day, and New Year's Day

Admission: Adults, $12.00; Seniors and Students, $9.50; New York City
public high school students with valid ID and Children under 12, Free;
Fridays from 6:00 PM–9:00 PM, pay what you wish. A one-day pass to
the Kaufman Astoria Studios Film & Video Gallery only is $6.00

Subway: 6 to 77th Street

Bus: M1, M2, M3, M4 to 74th Street

A leading advocate of twentieth and twenty-first-century
American art, the Whitney Museum of American Art was
founded in 1930 by Gertrude Vanderbilt Whitney expressly to
showcase the works of American artists who were overlooked by
other cultural institutions. The museum is a preeminent collection of American art and includes the entire artistic estate of
Edward Hopper, the largest public collection of works by
Alexander Calder, Louise Nevelson, and Lucas Samaras as well
as significant works by Jasper Johns, Donald Judd, Agnes
Martin, Bruce Nauman, Georgia O'Keefe, Claes Oldenburg,
Kiki Smith, and Andy Warhol, to name just a few. With its history of exhibiting the most promising and influential American
artists and provoking intense critical and public debate, the
Whitney's signature show, the Biennial, has become a measure of
the state of contemporary art in America today. In addition to
its world-renowned permanent collection of nearly 12,000 paint-

ings, sculptures, prints, drawings, and photographs, the museum presents several changing exhibitions as well as various programs and events for children and adults throughout the year.

Whitney Museum of American Art at Altria

120 Park Avenue at 42nd Street (Map 2)
917-663-2453
www.whitney.org/collection/altria

Open: Gallery: M–F, 11:00 AM–6:00 PM; Thursdays until 7:30 PM.
Sculpture Court: M–Sa, 7:30 AM–9:30 PM, Sundays and holidays, 11:00
AM–7:00 PM. Tours can be arranged by calling 917-663-2645
Admission: Free
Subway: 4, 5, 6, 7 and the Shuttle to Grand Central

The Whitney Museum of American Art at Altria is located in the street-level pedestrian plaza of the international headquarters of Altria Group, Inc., directly across the street from Grand Central Station. Altria Group has had an association with the Whitney for more than 30 years, having made substantial contributions to the operations of the museum and sponsoring several major exhibitions. Four exhibitions are organized annually in the 900-square-foot gallery, with an emphasis on solo exhibitions by contemporary living artists. Each year, one or two projects are also presented in the 5,200-square-foot Sculpture Court, a glass-enclosed atrium. A free brochure accompanies each exhibition, and gallery talks with the artists are organized regularly. Lunchtime gallery tours are offered every Wednesday and Friday at 1:00 PM. In addition to the exhibitions, the Whitney Museum at Altria produces Performance on 42nd, an ongoing series of free music, dance, theater, and performance art.

Wyckoff Farmhouse Museum

5816 Clarendon Road (Map 4)
Brooklyn
718-629-5400
www.wyckoffassociation.org

Open: Tu–Su, 10:00–4:00 PM. Closed Mondays
Admission: Adults, $2.00; Seniors (over 65) and Children under 18, $1.00
Group visits range from $3.00 to $7.00 depending on hands-on activities selected. All groups of six or more must have an appointment
Subway: 2, 5, D, Q to Newkirk Avenue. From there take the B8 bus east towards Brownsville to Beverly Road and East 59th Street. Walk one block south on East 59th to Clarendon Road and the park is across the street; A train to Utica Avenue/Malcolm X Boulevard and then take the B46 bus to Clarendon Road (local bus) or Avenue D (limited bus) and walk back one block to Clarendon Road, cross Utica Avenue and walk east on Clarendon about 9 blocks (crossing Kings Highway). The museum is in park on right-hand side at East 59th Street.

The Wyckoff House is New York City's oldest structure, built around 1652, and its first designated landmark. It is also a National Historic Landmark, designated in 1968. Pieter Claesen emigrated from the Netherlands in 1637 as an indentured servant and through connections to Peter Stuyvesant, Director-General of New Netherlands, settled in what was then known as New Amersfoort in 1652. Successive generations of Wyckoffs farmed the land until 1901. His descendants donated the house to the City in 1969, and after a major restoration it was opened as a museum in 1982. The museum aims to educate visitors about the life and customs of the diverse people of Brooklyn's Colonial farms. With household and farm activities, as well as special events scheduled throughout the year, visitors are taken back in time to see what Dutch and English agrarian life was like during the colonial period.

Highlights
1690s Dutch cradle from the Wyckoff family
Bills of sale for slaves from the early nineteenth century
Only surviving Dutch hearth in its original site

Yeshiva University Museum

15 West 16th Street between 5th & 6th Avenues (Map)

212-294-8330

www.yumuseum.org

Open: Tu, W, Th, Su, 11:00 AM–5:00 PM

Admission: Adults, $6.00; Seniors, Students, and Children 5–16, $4.00;
Children under 5, Free

Subway: 1, 9 to 14th or 18th Street; 4, 5, 6, N, R to Union Square

Located in the heart of Chelsea and housed in the Center for Jewish History, Yeshiva University Museum shares the building with four organizations devoted to Jewish research and culture. The center represents the largest repository of Jewish cultural history outside of Israel. The museum has four galleries, an exhibition arcade, an outdoor sculpture garden, and a children's workshop room as well as access to a 250-seat auditorium. The museum preserves and exhibits artifacts that represent the cultural, intellectual, and artistic achievement of more than 3,000 years of Jewish experience. Exhibitions are presented with an interdisciplinary focus to reflect the diversity of the collection of more than 8,000 artifacts. The museum also offers family craft workshops, films, concerts, and lectures.

Appendix

The following lists are thematic guides to the collections of the museums of New York City. All lists are in alphabetical order.

New York Essentials

American Museum of Natural History
The Frick Collection
Metropolitan Museum of Art
The Morgan Library & Museum
Museum of the City of New York
The Museum of Modern Art
The New-York Historical Society
The New York Public Library
Solomon R. Guggenheim Museum
Whitney Museum of American Art

Only in New York

Castle Clinton National Monument
The Cloisters
Ellis Island Immigration Museum and Statue of Liberty
Federal Hall National Monument
Fraunces Tavern Museum
Lower East Side Tenement Museum
Museum of American Finance
Municipal Archives of the City of New York
New York City Fire Museum
New York City Police Museum
New York Transit Museum
The Rose Museum at Carnegie Hall
The Skyscraper Museum

Ten Museums for Children

American Museum of Natural History
Brooklyn Children's Museum
Children's Museum of the Arts
Children's Museum of the Native American
Children's Museum of Manhattan
New York Hall of Science
Prospect Park Audubon Center
Queens County Farm Museum
Sony Wonder Technology Lab
Staten Island Children's Museum

Ten Museums — American History

The Conference House
Ellis Island Immigration Museum and Statue of Liberty
Federal Hall National Monument
Fraunces Tavern Museum
Historic Richmond Town
Morris-Jumel Mansion
Museum of American Finance
Old Stone House
South Street Seaport Museum
Theodore Roosevelt Birthplace

Ten Museums — Art & Architecture

Brooklyn Museum
Cooper-Hewitt, National Design Museum
The Frick Collection
Jacques Marchais Museum of Tibetan Art

Metropolitan Museum of Art
The Museum of Modern Art
National Academy Museum
The Skyscraper Museum
Solomon R. Guggenheim Museum
Whitney Museum of American Art

Ten Museums — Regional Interest

Bowne House
Dyckman Farmhouse Museum
Lower East Side Tenement Museum
Merchant's House Museum
Museum of the City of New York
New York City Fire Museum
New York City Police Museum
The New-York Historical Society
New York Transit Museum
Wyckoff Farmhouse Museum

Ten Museums — Science & Technology

American Museum of Natural History
American Numismatic Society
FDNY Fire Zone
Intrepid Sea-Air-Space Museum
Museum of the Moving Image
The Museum of Television and Radio
New York Hall of Science
Prospect Park Audubon Center
Queens County Farm Museum
Sony Wonder Technology Lab

Historic House Museums

Alice Austen House Museum
Bartow-Pell Mansion Museum, Carriage House and Gardens
Bowne House
The Conference House
Dyckman Farmhouse Museum
Garibaldi-Meucci Museum
Gracie Mansion
Historic Richmond Town
King Manor Museum
Kingsland Homestead
Lefferts Historic House
Louis Armstrong House
Merchant's House Museum
Morris-Jumel Mansion
Mount Vernon Hotel Museum & Garden
Old Stone House
Poe Cottage
Queens County Farm Museum
Theodore Roosevelt Birthplace
Valentine-Varian House
Van Cortlandt House Museum
Wyckoff Farmhouse Museum

Cultural Museums

Asia Society
The Bronx Museum of the Arts
Children's Museum of the Native American
El Museo del Barrio

Hebrew Union College–Jewish Institute of Religion

The Hispanic Society of America

Jacques Marchais Museum of Tibetan Art

Japan Society Gallery

The Jewish Museum

The Kurdish Library & Museum

Museum for African Art

Museum of Chinese in the Americas

Museum of Jewish Heritage

National Museum of the American Indian

Rubin Museum of Art

Schomburg Center for Research in Black Culture

The Studio Museum in Harlem

Ukrainian Museum

Yeshiva University Museum

Museums with Free Admission

The Anne Frank Center

Castle Clinton National Monument

FDNY Fire Zone

Federal Hall National Monument

Fisher Landau Center for Art

The Forbes Galleries

Hebrew Union College–Jewish Institute of Religion Museum

The Hispanic Society of America

The Kurdish Library & Museum

Lefferts Historic House

Municipal Archives of the City of New York

Museum at FIT

National Museum of the American Indian
The New York Public Library for the Performing Arts
The New York Public Library
Nicholas Roerich Museum
Queens County Farm Museum
The Rose Museum at Carnegie Hall
Schomburg Center for Research in Black Culture
Sony Wonder Technology Lab
Whitney Museum of American Art at Altria

Museums by Borough

BRONX

Bartow-Pell Mansion
The Bronx Museum of the Arts
Poe Cottage
Valentine-Varian House
Van Cortlandt House

BROOKLYN

Brooklyn Children's Museum
Brooklyn Historical Society
Brooklyn Museum
The Kurdish Library & Museum
Lefferts Historic House
New York Transit Museum
Old Stone House
Prospect Park Audubon Center
Wyckoff Farmhouse Museum

Manhattan

American Folk Art Museum
American Museum of Natural History
American Numismatic Society
The Anne Frank Center
Asia Society
Castle Clinton National Monument
Chelsea Art Museum
Children's Museum of the Arts
Children's Museum of Manhattan
Children's Museum of the Native American
The Cloisters
Cooper-Hewitt, National Design Museum
Dahesh Museum
Dyckman House
El Museo del Barrio
Ellis Island Immigration Museum and Statue of Liberty
FDNY Fire Zone
Federal Hall
The Forbes Galleries
Fraunces Tavern Museum
The Frick Collection
Gracie Mansion
Hebrew Union College–Jewish Institute of Religion Museum
The Hispanic Society of America
International Center for Photography
Intrepid Sea-Air-Space Museum
Japan Society Gallery
The Jewish Museum
Lower East Side Tenement Museum

Merchant's House Museum

Metropolitan Museum of Art

The Morgan Library & Museum

Morris-Jumel Mansion

Mount Vernon Hotel Museum & Garden

Municipal Archives of the City of New York

Museum at FIT

Museum of American Finance

Museum of Comic and Cartoon Art

Museum of Chinese in the Americas

Museum of Jewish Heritage

The Museum of Modern Art

The Museum of Sex

The Museum of Television and Radio

Museum of the City of New York

National Academy Museum

National Museum of the American Indian

National Sports Museum/Attraction

Neue Galerie New York

New York City Fire Museum

New York City Police Museum

The New-York Historical Society

The New York Public Library for the Performing Arts

The New York Public Library

Nicholas Roerich Museum

The Rose Museum at Carnegie Hall

Schomburg Center for Research in Black Culture

The Skyscraper Museum

Solomon R. Guggenheim Museum

Sony Wonder Technology Lab

South Street Seaport Museum

The Studio Museum in Harlem
Theodore Roosevelt House
Ukrainian Museum
Whitney Museum of American Art
Whitney Museum of American Art at Altria
Yeshiva University Museum

QUEENS

Bowne House
Fisher Landau Center for Art
King Manor Museum
Kingsland Homestead
Louis Armstrong House
Museum for African Art
Museum of the Moving Image
New York Hall of Science
The Noguchi Museum
P. S. 1 Contemporary Art Center
Queens County Farm Museum
Queens Museum of Art

STATEN ISLAND

Alice Austen House
The Conference House
Garibaldi-Meucci Museum
Historic Richmond Town
Jacques Marchais Museum of Tibetan Art
The Noble Maritime Collection
Staten Island Children's Museum
Staten Island Historical Society

Index of Alternative Museum Names

Abigail Adams Smith Museum, *see* Mount Vernon Hotel Museum & Garden

American Craft Museum, *see* Museum of Art & Design

American Indian Museum, *see* National Museum of the American Indian

Bronx Historical Society, *see* Valentine-Varian House

Carnegie Hall, *see* The Rose Museum at Carnegie Hall

Financial History Museum, *see* Museum of American Finance

Fire Museum, *see* New York City Fire Museum

Folk Art Museum, *see* American Folk Art Museum

Guggenheim, *see* Solomon R. Guggenheim Museum

MoMA, *see* The Museum of Modern Art

Natural History Museum, *see* American Museum of Natural History

Numismatic Society, *see* American Numismatic Society

Performing Arts Library, *see* The New York Public Library for the Performing Arts

Pierpont Morgan, *see* The Morgan Library & Museum

Police Museum, *see* New York City Police Museum

Queens Historical Society, *see* Kingsland Homestead

Sex Museum, *see* The Museum of Sex

Statue of Liberty, *see* Ellis Island Immigration Museum

Tenement Museum, *see* Lower East Side Tenement Museum

Transit Museum, *see* New York Transit Museum